Advance Praise for *The Courage to Teach: Exploring the Inner Landscape of a Teacher's Life*

"Parker Palmer has taught me more about learning and teaching than anyone else. His gift is to take us into the deepest places from which our work takes form, and illuminate that space with insight and courage that forever changes us. *The Courage to Teach* is for all of us—leaders, public officials, counselors, as well as teachers. It compassionately and insistently asks us to recognize that our capacity to do good work springs from our recognition of who we are. When we are firmly rooted in a true sense of self, we gain all the resources we require to do difficult but meaningful work. Our inner journeying makes our outer journey worthwhile. Our connectedness to who we are allows us to connect outward to all others."
　　—Margaret J. Wheatley, author, *Leadership and the New Science,*
　　and coauthor, *A Simpler Way*

"Parker Palmer is a Teacher in the truest sense of the word. In a series of insightful, eloquent, and spirit-filled books he has deepened our understanding of what it means to educate and to be educated. No one has done more to raise our standards or deepen our insight about the connections between education, community, and spirituality."
　　—David W. Orr, chair, Environmental Studies Program,
　　Oberlin College, and author, *Earth in Mind: On Education,*
　　Environment, and the Human Prospect

"This book is good news—not just for classroom teachers and educators, but for all of us who are committed to the healing of our world. Any activist worth her salt, any effective organizer for social change, needs the same blend of humility and confidence, the same respect for the human mystery, the same crazy readiness to risk, that characterizes a great teacher. And this is Parker Palmer, and this is what he brings to us."
　　—Joanna Macy, author, *World as Lover, World as Self*

"More than any thinker who has inspired me, Parker Palmer speaks from and to the heart. His writing is suffused with a rare mix of rigor and elegance, of passion and precision, of wisdom and humanity. His book is a gift to all who love teaching and learning, especially those whose love is intermingled with struggle and pain.

The questions it poses are universal and yet personal, moving from the teacher's search for integrity to the large-scale project of educational reform. The questions could not be more urgent: How can we keep deepening our capacity to teach and to learn? How can we preserve the joy and the love of teaching? How can we grow as teachers, and as human beings, feed the yearning that we have for connectedness, nurture forms of community that support teaching and learning?

The Courage to Teach approaches these questions along three paths, all intertwined: intellectual, emotional, and spiritual. It charts the way with a vision for education that illuminates all three. It is a profoundly satisfying feast of a book."

—Diana Chapman Walsh, president, Wellesley College

"*The Courage to Teach* is a profoundly moving, utterly passionate, and inspired articulation of the call to, and the pain and joy of, teaching. It is must reading for any and every teacher, at any level. It wakes us up to the enormity of the challenge and to the adequacy of our own generativity and genius, if we can but listen to and honor the calling moment by moment. Parker Palmer reminds us that teaching is nothing less than the inner work of a lifetime, a love affair with life itself, both beyond subject and intimate with subject. He shows us how authentic teaching has to be an ongoing relational process, a practice of exquisite and wide-ranging attention refining teacher and student—including the student in the teacher and the teacher in the student—in the flames of solitary and collective inquiry and in a courageous commitment to seeing, knowing, sharing, and belonging: in a word, to truth."

—Jon Kabat-Zinn, author, *Wherever You Go, There You Are,*
and coauthor, *Everyday Blessings*

"Evokes the heart of what teachers really do, and does so in a vivid, compelling, and soulful way."

—Robert Coles

"To go on this journey with Parker Palmer into the uncharted territory of 'the self' in teaching is not only to experience the joy of viewing teaching from a thrilling new perspective. It is also to be in the presence of a great teacher who, by sharing himself so openly and honestly, engages us in the very kind of teaching he so eloquently describes."

—Russ Edgerton, director of educational programs,
Pew Charitable Trusts, and past president, American
Association for Higher Education

OTHER BOOKS BY PARKER J. PALMER

The Active Life

The Company of Strangers

Caring for the Commonweal (coeditor)

The Promise of Paradox

To Know As We Are Known

The Courage
to Teach

The Courage
to Teach

EXPLORING THE INNER LANDSCAPE OF
A TEACHER'S LIFE

Parker J. Palmer

JOSSEY-BASS
A Wiley Company
www.josseybass.com

Published by

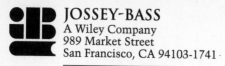 **JOSSEY-BASS**
A Wiley Company
989 Market Street
San Francisco, CA 94103-1741

www.josseybass.com

Jossey-Bass books and products are available through most bookstores. To contact Jossey-Bass directly, call (888) 378-2537, fax to (800) 605-2665, or visit our website at www.josseybass.com.

Substantial discounts on bulk quantities of Jossey-Bass books are available to corporations, professional associations, and other organizations. For details and discount information, contact the special sales department at Jossey-Bass.

We at Jossey-Bass strive to use the most environmentally sensitive paper stocks available to us. Our publications are printed on acid-free recycled stock whenever possible, and our paper always meets or exceeds minimum GPO and EPA requirements.

Credits are on p. 201.

Library of Congress Cataloging-in-Publication Data

Palmer, Parker J.
   The courage to teach : exploring the inner landscape of a teacher's life / Parker J. Palmer. — 1st ed.
      p.   cm.
   Includes bibliographical references and index.
   ISBN 0-7879-1058-9 (cloth : acid-free paper)
   1. Teachers. 2. Teaching. 3. Learning. I. Title.
LB1775.P25 1998
371.102—DC21   97-21161

FIRST EDITION
HB Printing   20 19 18 17 16 15 14 13

Contents

For Sharon

and in grateful memory of my father
Max J. Palmer
(1912–1994)

Gratitudes

In 1983, I published *To Know As We Are Known: Education as a Spiritual Journey.* That book has opened opportunities for me to meet and work with teachers in diverse settings across the country: colleges and universities, public schools, continuing education programs, retreat centers, religious institutions, and "learning organizations" of many sorts—businesses, foundations, and groups working for social change.

In dialogue with this remarkable array of educators, I was challenged to write a book that would go beyond *To Know As We Are Known* in two respects: it would have both a sustained focus on the practice of teaching and an approach to the inner life that is open to the varied paths of the devoted teachers I have met. *The Courage to Teach* is that book, and I thank the kindred spirits who have encouraged me along the way.

My special thanks go to Robert F. Lehman, president of the Fetzer Institute, where I am senior adviser. Through a series of institute projects, he made it possible for me to lay down my travels long enough to finish this book. Even more generous has been his faithful companionship on the inner journey from which this book emerges. Rob Lehman understands the inner life and its impact on the world of action at a depth rare and heartening. For his insight, friendship, and witness I am profoundly grateful.

Working with the Fetzer Institute has enlarged my experience of education. My own teaching has been primarily in universities and adult study programs, and most of the stories in this book come from those worlds. But over the past five years, I have gained some insights into the lives of K–12 teachers by helping Fetzer create the Teacher Formation Program, a two-year sequence of renewal retreats for teachers in public schools. The program currently has sites in Illinois, Maryland, Michigan, South Carolina, and Washington State, and as this book goes to press, the Fetzer Institute is establishing a national Center for Teacher Formation to develop additional K–12 sites (and eventually, perhaps, to create a renewal program for college faculty as well).[1]

From 1994 to 1996, I led the first Teacher Formation group. My gratitude goes to the inspiring Michigan public school teachers who made that experiment so successful: Maggie Adams, Jack Bender, Mark Bond, Lauri Bowersox, Margaret Ells, Richard Fowler, Linda Hamel, Eleanor Hayward, Marianne Houston, Katherine Kennedy, Cheri McLoughan, Michael Perry, Linda Powell, Toni Rostami, Rick Serafini, Gerald Thompson, and Marcia Weinhold.

I am grateful, too, for the people who are giving the Teacher Formation Program a larger and continuing life. They include Judy Brown, Tony Chambers, Charlie Glasser, Eleanor Greenslade, Sally Hare, Marianne Houston, Marcy Jackson, Rick Jackson, Mickey Olivanti, Megan Scribner, David Sluyter, and Penny Williamson, my friends and gifted partners in program development; the staff of the Fetzer Institute, whose devotion and hard work—answering calls, writing memos, issuing checks, cleaning rooms, caring for the grounds, and putting food on the table—has kept the program afloat; and the trustees of the institute who believe in this work and have backed it: Janis Claflin, Bruce Fetzer, Wink Franklin, Lynne Twist, Frances Vaughan, Jeremy Waletzky, and Judith Skutch Whitson (trustee emerita).

For the past decade I have worked independently. Though I teach constantly—in seminars and workshops and retreats, "classrooms" of many sorts—I no longer teach in traditional settings with the same students for a semester or more, as I did earlier in my career at Beloit College, Georgetown University, and Pendle Hill, the Quaker living-learning community.

So I was grateful to be appointed the Eli Lilly Visiting Professor at Berea College in Berea, Kentucky, in 1993–94. During that year, I was rebaptized into the realities of college teaching, and I wrote the first draft of this book. My special thanks go to Phyllis Hughes, Libby Jones, Larry Shinn, the late John Stephenson, and members of the Berea Friends Meeting for encouraging me to grow in my vocation.

I also thank my friends at the American Association of Higher Education (AAHE), where I serve as senior associate: Russ Edgerton (past president of AAHE, now director of educational programs at the Pew Charitable Trusts), Lou Albert, Pat Hutchings, and Ted Marchese. For a decade and more, they have encouraged and helped shape my work, giving me access to an extraordinary community of discourse that I could never have discovered on my own.

Most of the work on this book was done in 1996–97, and during that time I was blessed with four superb editors. All of them helped make this book better than it would have been had I written it alone.

Sarah Polster and Sheryl Fullerton were my editors at Jossey-Bass Publishers. I thank them for supporting me and challenging me in the right proportions and at the right times.

Mark Nepo is a poet, essayist, teacher, and editor extraordinaire. He read every word I wrote with care, commented on most of them with passion, pro and con, and tried to evoke my voice instead of imposing his own. For helping me find vessels to hold the treasure and for showing me treasure I had not seen, he has my endless thanks.

Sharon Palmer has lovingly shared all the ups and downs of this project and, with her keen eye and good heart, has worked to keep my prose lucid and my spirit whole. The dedication of this book only begins to suggest the depth of my gratitude to her—and to my father, the best man I have ever known.

Madison, Wisconsin   Parker J. Palmer
September 1997

The Courage
to Teach

Introduction

Teaching from Within

Ah, not to be cut off,
not through the slightest partition
shut out from the law of the stars.
The inner—what is it?
if not intensified sky,
hurled through with birds and deep
with the winds of homecoming.

—Rainer Maria Rilke, "[Ah, not to be cut off]"[1]

WE TEACH WHO WE ARE

I am a teacher at heart, and there are moments in the classroom when I can hardly hold the joy. When my students and I discover uncharted territory to explore, when the pathway out of a thicket opens up before us, when our experience is illumined by the lightning-life of the mind—then teaching is the finest work I know.

But at other moments, the classroom is so lifeless or painful or confused—and I am so powerless to do anything about it—that my claim to be a teacher seems a transparent sham. Then the enemy is everywhere: in those students from some alien planet, in that subject I thought I knew, and in the personal pathology that keeps me earning my living this way. What a fool I was to imagine that I had mastered this occult art—harder to divine than tea leaves and impossible for mortals to do even passably well!

If you are a teacher who never has bad days, or who has them but does not care, this book is not for you. This book is for teachers who have good days and bad, and whose bad days bring the suffering that comes only from something one loves. It is for teachers who refuse to harden their hearts because they love learners, learning, and the teaching life.

When you love your work that much—and many teachers do—the only way to get out of trouble is to go deeper in. We must enter, not evade, the tangles of teaching so we can understand them better and negotiate them with more grace, not only to guard our own spirits but also to serve our students well.

Those tangles have three important sources. The first two are commonplace, but the third, and most fundamental, is rarely given its due. First, the subjects we teach are as large and complex as life, so our knowledge of them is always flawed and partial. No matter how we devote ourselves to reading and research, teaching requires a command of content that always eludes our grasp. Second, the students we teach are larger than life and even more complex. To see them clearly and see them whole, and respond to them wisely in the moment, requires a fusion of Freud and Solomon that few of us achieve.

If students and subjects accounted for all the complexities of teaching, our standard ways of coping would do—keep up with our fields as best we can and learn enough techniques to stay ahead of the student psyche. But there is another reason for these complexities: we teach who we are.

Teaching, like any truly human activity, emerges from one's inwardness, for better or worse. As I teach, I project the condition of my soul onto my students, my subject, and our way of being together. The entanglements I experience in the classroom are often no more or less than the convolutions of my inner life. Viewed from this angle, teaching holds a mirror to the soul. If I am willing to look in that mirror and not run from what I see, I have a chance to gain self-knowledge—and knowing myself is as crucial to good teaching as knowing my students and my subject.

In fact, knowing my students and my subject depends heavily on self-knowledge. When I do not know myself, I cannot know who my students are. I will see them through a glass darkly, in the shadows of my unexamined life—and when I cannot see them clearly, I cannot teach them well. When I do not know myself, I cannot know my subject—not at the deepest levels of embodied, personal meaning. I will know it only abstractly, from a distance, a congeries of concepts as far removed from the world as I am from personal truth.

The work required to "know thyself" is neither selfish nor narcissistic. Whatever self-knowledge we attain as teachers will serve our students and our scholarship well. Good teaching requires self-knowledge: it is a secret hidden in plain sight.

LANDSCAPES INNER AND OUTER

This book explores the teacher's inner life, but it also raises a question that goes beyond the solitude of the teacher's soul: How can the teacher's selfhood become a legitimate topic in education and in our public dialogues on educational reform?

Teaching and learning are critical to our individual and collective survival and to the quality of our lives. The pace of change has us snarled in complexities, confusions, and conflicts that will diminish us, or do us in, if we do not enlarge our capacity to teach and to learn. At the same time, teacher-bashing has become a popular sport. Panic-stricken by the demands of our day, we need scapegoats for the problems we cannot solve and the sins we cannot bear.

Teachers make an easy target, for they are such a common species and so powerless to strike back. We blame teachers for being unable to cure social ills that no one knows how to treat; we insist that they instantly adopt whatever "solution" has most recently been concocted by our national panacea machine; and in the process, we demoralize, even paralyze, the very teachers who could help us find our way.

In our rush to reform education, we have forgotten a simple truth: reform will never be achieved by renewing appropriations, restructuring schools, rewriting curricula, and revising texts if we continue to demean and dishearten the human resource called the teacher on whom so much depends. Teachers must be better compensated, freed from bureaucratic harassment, given a role in academic governance, and provided with the best possible methods and materials. But none of that will transform education if we fail to cherish—and challenge—the human heart that is the source of good teaching.

We are now engaged in a crucial public conversation about educational reform, but a conversation is only as good as the questions it entertains. This book raises a question about teaching that goes unasked in our national dialogue—and often goes unasked even in the places where teachers are educated and employed. But it should be asked wherever good teaching is at stake, for it honors and challenges the teacher's heart, and it invites a deeper inquiry than our traditional questions do:

- The question we most commonly ask is the "what" question—what subjects shall we teach?
- When the conversation goes a bit deeper, we ask the "how" question—what methods and techniques are required to teach well?
- Occasionally, when it goes deeper still, we ask the "why" question—for what purpose and to what ends do we teach?
- But seldom, if ever, do we ask the "who" question—who is the self that teaches? How does the quality of my selfhood form—or deform—the way I relate to my students, my subject, my colleagues, my world? How can educational institutions sustain and deepen the selfhood from which good teaching comes?

I have no quarrel with the what or how or why questions—except when they are posed as the only questions worth asking. All of them can yield important insights into teaching and learning. But none of them opens up the territory I want to explore in this book: the inner landscape of the teaching self.

To chart that landscape fully, three important paths must be taken—intellectual, emotional, and spiritual—and none can be ignored. Reduce teaching to intellect, and it becomes a cold abstraction; reduce it to emotions, and it becomes narcissistic; reduce it to the spiritual, and it loses its anchor to the world. Intellect, emotion, and spirit depend on one another for wholeness. They are interwoven in the human self and in education at its best, and I have tried to interweave them in this book as well.

By *intellectual* I mean the way we think about teaching and learning—the form and content of our concepts of how people know and learn, of the nature of our students and our subjects. By *emotional* I mean the way we and our students feel as we teach and learn—feelings that can either enlarge or diminish the exchange between us. By *spiritual* I mean the diverse ways we answer the heart's longing to be connected with the largeness of life—a longing that animates love and work, especially the work called teaching.

Rainer Maria Rilke gives voice to that longing in the poem at the head of this introduction: "Ah, not to be cut off . . ." He suggests that the spiritual quest for connectedness, rightly understood, will lead us out from the hidden heart into the vast and visible world: "The inner—what is it?/if not intensified sky,/hurled through with birds and deep/with the winds of homecoming."

With striking imagery, Rilke offers us a mystic's map of wholeness, where inner and outer reality flow seamlessly into each other, like the ever-merging surfaces of a Möbius strip, endlessly co-creating us and the world we inhabit. Though this book is grounded in the teacher's inner terrain, it constantly segues into the outer forms of community that teaching and learning require. The inward quest for communion becomes a quest for outward relationship: at home in our own souls, we become more at home with each other.

My concern for the inner landscape of teaching may seem indulgent, even irrelevant, at a time when many teachers are struggling simply to survive. Wouldn't it be more practical, I am sometimes asked, to offer tips, tricks, and techniques for staying alive in the classroom, things that ordinary teachers can use in everyday life?

The question puzzles me, because for twenty years I have made practical use of the approach taken in this book, leading workshops and retreats for educators of all sorts. I have worked with countless teachers, and many of them have confirmed my own experience: as important as methods may be, the most practical thing we can achieve in any kind of work is insight into what is happening inside us as we do it. The more familiar we are with our inner terrain, the more surefooted our teaching—and living—becomes.

I have heard that in the training of therapists, which involves much practical technique, there is this saying: "Technique is what you use until the therapist arrives." Good methods can help a therapist find a way into the client's dilemma, but good therapy does not begin until the real-life therapist joins with the real life of the client.

Technique is what teachers use until the real teacher arrives, and this book is about helping that teacher show up. Yet even if it is true that inner work has practical outcomes for individuals, the question of practicality arises in another form: How can educational institutions support the teacher's inner life, and should they be expected to do so?

That question is worthy of a thoughtful answer, so Chapter VI is devoted to it. For the moment, I will turn the question around: How can schools educate students if they fail to support the teacher's inner life? To educate is to guide students on an inner journey toward more truthful ways of seeing and being in the world. How can schools perform their mission without encouraging the guides to scout out that inner terrain?

A SELDOM-TAKEN TRAIL

My focus on the teacher may seem passé to people who believe that education will never be reformed until we stop worrying about teaching and focus on learning instead.

I have no question that students who learn, not professors who perform, is what teaching is all about: students who learn are the finest fruit of teachers who teach. Nor do I doubt that students learn in diverse and wondrous ways, including ways that bypass the teacher in the classroom and ways that require neither a classroom nor a teacher!

But I am also clear that in lecture halls, seminar rooms, field settings, labs, and even electronic classrooms—the places where most people receive most of their formal education—teachers possess the power to create conditions that can help students learn a great deal—or keep them from learning much at all. Teaching is the intentional act of creating those conditions, and good teaching requires that we understand the inner sources of both the intent and the act.

Most of my teaching has been in colleges and programs for older adults, but in recent years I have been enriched by working with public school teachers, from kindergarten through the twelfth grade. I have learned much from my K–12 colleagues, including these two things: teachers at all levels of education have more in common than we think, and we should not be so glib about which level we call "higher."

Kindergarten teachers often understand the craft better than those of us with Ph.D.'s, perhaps because students in the "lower" grades are like the child in "The Emperor's New Clothes." They do not care what graduate school you attended, who chaired your dissertation committee, or how many books you have written, but they quickly sense whether you are real, and they respond accordingly. The discerning innocence of young children deepens my conviction that at every level of education, the selfhood of the teacher is key.

"Who is the self that teaches?" is the question at the heart of this book—though answering that question in print has been more challenging than I imagined. In writing and rewriting this book many times over the past five years, I have learned how tempting it is to stay with the "whats" and "hows" and "whys": those questions are more easily answered in prose and translated into proposals for fundable programs!

But I have persisted with the "who" question because it marks a seldom-taken trail in the quest for educational reform, a trail toward the recovery of the inner resources that good teaching always requires. Real reform is so badly needed—and we have restructured education so often without reaching that distant dream—that we should be sending expeditionary parties down every trail we can find.

I have persisted for another reason closer to the bone: "Who is the self that teaches?" is the question at the heart of my own vocation. I believe it is the most fundamental question we can ask about teaching and those who teach—for the sake of learning and those who learn. By addressing it openly and honestly, alone and together, we can serve our students more faithfully, enhance our own well-being, make common cause with colleagues, and help education bring more light and life to the world.

Chapter I

The Heart of a Teacher
Identity and Integrity in Teaching

Now I become myself. It's taken
Time, many years and places;
I have been dissolved and shaken,
Worn other people's faces . . .

—MAY SARTON, "NOW I BECOME MYSELF"[1]

TEACHING BEYOND TECHNIQUE

Not long before I started this book, as summer took a slow turn toward fall, I walked into a college classroom and into my third decade of teaching.

I went to class that day grateful for another chance to teach; teaching engages my soul as much as any work I know. But I came home that evening convinced once again that I will never master this baffling vocation. Annoyed with some of my students and embarrassed by my own blunders, I pondered a recurring question: Might it be possible, at my age, to find a new line of work, maybe even something I know how to do?

The students in my first section were silent as monks. Despite my shameless pleading, I could not buy a response from them, and I soon found myself sinking into one of my oldest phobias: I must be very boring to anesthetize, so quickly, these young people who only moments earlier had been alive with hallway chatter.

In the second section they talked, but the talk flared into conflict as one student insisted that the concerns of another student were "petty" and did not deserve attention. I masked my irritation and urged open listening to diverse views, but the air was already polluted, and the dialogue died. That, of course, sank me into another ancient angst: how awkward I am at dealing with conflict when my students decide to start talking!

I have taught thousands of students, attended many seminars on teaching, watched others teach, read about teaching, and reflected on my own experience. My stockpile of methods is substantial. But when I walk into a new class, it is as if I am starting over. My problems are perennial, familiar to all teachers. Still, they take me by surprise, and my responses to them—though outwardly smoother with each year—feel almost as fumbling as they did when I was a novice.

After three decades of trying to learn my craft, every class comes down to this: my students and I, face to face, engaged in an ancient and exacting exchange called education. The techniques I have mastered do not disappear, but neither do they suffice. Face to face with my students, only one resource is at my immediate command: my identity, my selfhood, my sense of this "I" who teaches—without which I have no sense of the "Thou" who learns.

This book builds on a simple premise: *good teaching cannot be reduced to technique; good teaching comes from the identity and integrity of the teacher.*

The premise is simple, but its implications are not. It will take time to unfold what I do and do not mean by those words. But here is one way to put it: in every class I teach, my ability to connect with my students, and to connect them with the subject, depends less on the methods I use than on the degree to which I know and trust my selfhood—and am willing to make it available and vulnerable in the service of learning.

My evidence for this claim comes, in part, from years of asking students to tell me about their good teachers. Listening to those stories, it becomes impossible to claim that all good teachers use similar techniques: some lecture nonstop and others speak very little; some stay close to their material and others loose the imagination; some teach with the carrot and others with the stick.

But in every story I have heard, good teachers share one trait: a strong sense of personal identity infuses their work. "Dr. A is really *there* when she teaches," a student tells me, or "Mr. B has such enthusiasm for his subject," or "You can tell that this is really Prof. C's life."

One student I heard about said she could not describe her good teachers because they differed so greatly, one from another. But she could describe her bad teachers because they were all the same: "Their words float somewhere in front of their faces, like the balloon speech in cartoons."

With one remarkable image she said it all. Bad teachers distance themselves from the subject they are teaching—and in the process, from their students. Good teachers join self and subject and students in the fabric of life.

Good teachers possess a capacity for connectedness. They are able to weave a complex web of connections among themselves, their subjects, and their students so that students can learn to weave a world for themselves. The methods used by these weavers vary widely: lectures, Socratic dialogues, laboratory experiments, collaborative problem solving, creative chaos. The connections made by good teachers are held not in their methods but in their hearts— meaning *heart* in its ancient sense, as the place where intellect and emotion and spirit and will converge in the human self.

As good teachers weave the fabric that joins them with students and subjects, the heart is the loom on which the threads are tied, the tension is held, the shuttle flies, and the fabric is stretched tight. Small wonder, then, that teaching tugs at the heart, opens the heart, even breaks the heart—and the more one loves teaching, the more heartbreaking it can be. The courage to teach is the courage to keep one's heart open in those very moments when the heart is asked to hold more than it is able so that teacher and students and subject can be woven into the fabric of community that learning, and living, require.

If teaching cannot be reduced to technique, it is both good news and bad. The good news is that we no longer need suffer the boredom many of us feel when teaching is approached as a question of "how to do it." We rarely talk with each other about teaching at any depth—and why should we when we have nothing more than "tips, tricks, and techniques" to discuss? That kind of talk fails to touch the heart of a teacher's experience.

The good news gets even better. If teaching cannot be reduced to technique, I no longer need suffer the pain of having my peculiar gift as a teacher crammed into the Procrustean bed of someone else's method and the standards prescribed by it. That pain is felt throughout education today as we glorify the method *du jour,* leaving people who teach differently feeling devalued, forcing them to measure up to norms not their own.

I will never forget one professor who, moments before I was to start a workshop on teaching, unloaded years of pent-up workshop animus on me: "I am an organic chemist. Are you going to spend the next two days telling me that I am supposed to teach organic chemistry through role playing?" We must find an approach to teaching that respects the diversity of teachers and subjects, which methodological reductionism fails to do.

The good news is very good, but the bad news is daunting. If identity and integrity are more fundamental to good teaching than technique—and if we want to grow as teachers—we must do something alien to academic culture: we must talk to each other about our inner lives—risky stuff in a profession that fears the personal and seeks safety in the technical, the distant, the abstract.

I was reminded of that fear recently as I listened to a group of faculty argue about what to do when students share personal experiences in class—experiences that are related to the themes of the course but that some professors regard as "more suited to a therapy session than to a college classroom."

The house soon divided along predictable lines. On one side were the scholars, insisting that the subject is primary and must never be compromised for the sake of the students' lives. On the other side were the student-centered folks, insisting that the lives of students must always come first even if it means that the subject gets shortchanged. The more vigorously these camps promoted their polarized ideas, the more antagonistic they became—and the less they learned about pedagogy or about themselves.

The gap between these views seems unbridgeable—until we understand what creates it. At bottom, these professors were not debating teaching techniques. They were revealing the diversity of identity and integrity among themselves, saying, in various ways, "Here are my own limits and potentials when it comes to dealing with the relation between the subject and my students' lives."

If we stopped lobbing pedagogical points at each other and spoke about *who we are* as teachers, a remarkable thing might happen: identity and integrity might grow within us and among us, instead of hardening as they do when we defend our fixed positions from the foxholes of the pedagogy wars.

TEACHING AND TRUE SELF

The claim that good teaching comes from the identity and integrity of the teacher might sound like a truism, and a pious one at that: good teaching comes from good people.

But by identity and integrity I do not mean only our noble features, or the good deeds we do, or the brave faces we wear to conceal our confusions and complexities. Identity and integrity have as much to do with our shadows and limits, our wounds and fears, as with our strengths and potentials.

By *identity* I mean an evolving nexus where all the forces that constitute my life converge in the mystery of self: my genetic makeup, the nature of the man and woman who gave me life, the culture in which I was raised, people who have sustained me and people who have done me harm, the good and ill I have done to others and to myself, the experience of love and suffering—and much, much more. In the midst of that complex field, identity is a moving intersection of the inner and outer forces that make me who I am, converging in the irreducible mystery of being human.

By *integrity* I mean whatever wholeness I am able to find within that nexus as its vectors form and re-form the pattern of my life. Integrity requires that I discern what is integral to my selfhood, what fits and what does not—and that I choose life-giving ways of relating to the forces that converge within me: Do I welcome them or fear them, embrace them or reject them, move with them or against them? By choosing integrity, I become more whole, but wholeness does not mean perfection. It means becoming more real by acknowledging the whole of who I am.

Identity and integrity are not the granite from which fictional heroes are hewn. They are subtle dimensions of the complex, demanding, and lifelong process of self-discovery. *Identity* lies in the intersection of the diverse forces that make up my life, and *integrity* lies in relating to those forces in ways that bring me wholeness and life rather than fragmentation and death.

13

Those are my definitions—but try as I might to refine them, they always come out too pat. Identity and integrity can never be fully named or known by anyone, including the person who bears them. They constitute that familiar strangeness we take with us to the grave, elusive realities that can be caught only occasionally out of the corner of the eye.

Stories are the best way to portray realities of this sort, so here is a tale of two teachers, a tale based on people I have known, whose lives tell me more about the subtleties of identity and integrity than any theory could.

Alan and Eric were born into two different families of skilled craftspeople, rural folk with little formal schooling but gifted in the manual arts. Both boys evinced this gift from childhood onward, and as each grew in the skill of working with his hands, each developed a sense of self in which the pride of craft was key.

The two shared another gift as well: both excelled in school and became the first in their working-class families to go to college. Both did well as undergraduates, both were admitted to graduate school, both earned doctorates, and both chose academic careers.

But here their paths diverged. Though the gift of craft was central in both men's sense of self, Alan was able to weave that gift into his academic vocation, whereas the fabric of Eric's life unraveled early on.

Catapulted from his rural community into an elite private college at age eighteen, Eric suffered culture shock and never overcame it. He was insecure with fellow students and, later, with academic colleagues who came from backgrounds he saw as more "cultured" than his own. He learned to speak and act like an intellectual, but he always felt fraudulent among people who were, in his eyes, to the manor born.

But insecurity neither altered Eric's course nor drew him into self-reflection. Instead, he bullied his way into professional life on the theory that the best defense is a good offense. He made pronouncements rather than probes. He listened for weaknesses rather than strengths in what other people said. He argued with anyone about anything—and responded with veiled contempt to whatever was said in return.

In the classroom, Eric was critical and judgmental, quick to put down the "stupid question," adept at trapping students with trick questions of his own, then merciless in mocking wrong answers. He seemed driven by a need to inflict on his students the same wound that academic life had inflicted on him—the wound of being embarrassed by some essential part of one's self.

But when Eric went home to his workbench and lost himself in craft, he found himself as well. He became warm and welcoming, at home in the world and glad to extend hospitality to others. Reconnected with his roots, centered in his true self, he was able to reclaim a quiet and confident core—which he quickly lost as soon as he returned to campus.

Alan's is a different story. His leap from countryside to campus did not induce culture shock, in part because he attended a land-grant university where many students had backgrounds much like his own. He was not driven to hide his gift but was able to honor and transform it by turning it toward things academic: he brought to his study, and later to his teaching and research, the same sense of craft that his ancestors brought to their work with metal and wood.

Watching Alan teach, you felt that you were watching a craftsman at work—and if you knew his history, you understood that this feeling was more than metaphor. In his lectures, every move Alan made was informed by attention to detail and respect for the materials at hand; he connected ideas with the precision of dovetail joinery and finished the job with a polished summary.

But the power of Alan's teaching went well beyond crafted performance. His students knew that Alan would extend himself with great generosity to any of them who wanted to become an apprentice in his field, just as the elders in his own family had extended themselves to help young Alan grow in his original craft.

Alan taught from an undivided self—an integral state of being central to good teaching and a concept central to this book. In the undivided self, every major thread of one's life experience is honored, creating a weave of such coherence and strength that it can hold students and subject as well as self. Such a self, inwardly integrated, is able to make the outward connections on which good teaching depends.

But Eric failed to weave the central strand of his identity into his academic vocation. His was a self divided, engaged in a civil war. He projected that inner warfare onto the outer world, and his teaching devolved into combat instead of craft. The divided self will always distance itself from others, and may even try to destroy them, to defend its fragile identity.

If Eric had not been alienated as an undergraduate—or if his alienation had led to self-reflection instead of self-defense—it is possible that he, like Alan, could have found integrity in his academic vocation, could have woven the major strands of his identity into his work. But part of the mystery of selfhood is the fact that one size does not fit all: what is integral to one person lacks integrity for another. Throughout his life there were persistent clues that academia was not a life-giving choice for Eric, not a context in which his true self could emerge healthy and whole, not a vocation integral to his unique nature.

The self is not infinitely elastic—it has potentials and it has limits. If the work we do lacks integrity for us, then we, the work, and the people we do it with will suffer. Alan's self was enlarged by his academic vocation, and the work he did was a joy to behold. Eric's self was diminished by his encounter with academia, and choosing a different vocation might have been his only way to recover integrity lost.

Gandhi called his life "experiments with truth," and experimenting in the complex field of forces that bear on our lives is how we learn more about our integrity.[2] We learn experimentally that we thrive on some connections and wither with others, that we enhance our integrity by choosing relationships that give us life and violate it by assenting to those that do not.

Experimentation is risky. We rarely know in advance what will give us life and what will sap life away. But if we want to deepen our understanding of our own integrity, experiment we must—and then be willing to make choices as we view the experimental results.

"All real living is meeting," said Martin Buber, and teaching is endless meeting.[3] Staying open to new meetings, trying to distinguish those that have integrity from those that do not, is a tiring and sometimes frightening task. I am often tempted to protect my sense of self behind barricades of status or role, to withhold myself from colleagues or students or ideas and from the collisions we will surely have.

When I succumb to that temptation, my identity and integrity are diminished—and I lose the heart to teach.

When Teachers Lose Heart

Many of us became teachers for reasons of the heart, animated by a passion for some subject and for helping people learn. But many of us lose heart as the years of teaching go by. How can we take heart in teaching once more so that we can, as good teachers always do, give heart to our students?

We lose heart, in part, because teaching is a daily exercise in vulnerability. I need not reveal personal secrets to feel naked in front of a class. I need only parse a sentence or work a proof on the board while my students doze off or pass notes. No matter how technical my subject may be, the things I teach are things I care about—and what I care about helps define my selfhood.

Unlike many professions, teaching is always done at the dangerous intersection of personal and public life. A good therapist must work in a personal way, but never publicly: the therapist who reveals as much as a client's name is derelict. A good trial lawyer must work in a public forum but remain unswayed by personal opinion: the lawyer who allows private feelings about a client's guilt to weaken the client's defense is guilty of malpractice.

But a good teacher must stand where personal and public meet, dealing with the thundering flow of traffic at an intersection where "weaving a web of connectedness" feels more like crossing a freeway on foot. As we try to connect ourselves and our subjects with our students, we make ourselves, as well as our subjects, vulnerable to indifference, judgment, ridicule.

To reduce our vulnerability, we disconnect from students, from subjects, and even from ourselves. We build a wall between inner truth and outer performance, and we play-act the teacher's part. Our words, spoken at remove from our hearts, become "the balloon speech in cartoons," and we become caricatures of ourselves. We distance ourselves from students and subject to minimize the danger—forgetting that distance makes life more dangerous still by isolating the self.

This "self-protective" split of personhood from practice is encouraged by an academic culture that distrusts personal truth. Though the academy claims to value multiple modes of knowing, it honors only one—an "objective" way of knowing that takes us into the "real" world by taking us "out of ourselves."

In this culture, objective facts are regarded as pure, while subjective feelings are suspect and sullied. In this culture, the self is not a source to be tapped but a danger to be suppressed, not a potential to be fulfilled but an obstacle to be overcome. In this culture, the pathology of speech disconnected from self is regarded, and rewarded, as a virtue.

If my sketch of the academic bias against selfhood seems overdone, here is a story from a class that I taught at a large university some years ago.

I assigned my students a series of brief analytical essays involving themes in the texts we were going to be reading. Then I assigned a parallel series of autobiographical sketches, related to those themes, so that my students could see connections between the textbook concepts and their own lives.

After the first class, a student came up to me and inquired, "In those autobiographical essays you asked us to write, is it OK to use the word 'I'?"

I did not know whether to laugh or cry—but I knew that my response would have considerable impact on a young man who had just opened himself to ridicule. I told him that not only could he use the word "I," but I hoped he would use it freely and often. Then I asked what had led to his question.

"I'm a history major," he said, "and each time I use 'I' in a paper, they knock off half a grade."

The academic bias against subjectivity not only forces our students to write poorly ("It is believed . . . ," instead of "I believe . . .") but also deforms their thinking about themselves and their world. In a single stroke, we delude our students into thinking that bad prose can turn opinions into facts, and we alienate them from their own inner lives.

Faculty often complain that students have no regard for the gifts of insight and understanding that are the true payoff of education—they care only about short-term outcomes in the "real" world: "Will this major get me a job?" "How will this assignment be useful in 'real' life?"

But those are not the questions deep in our students' hearts. They are merely the questions they have been taught to ask, not only by tuition-paying parents who want their children to be employable but also by an academic culture that distrusts and devalues inner reality. Of course our students are cynical about the inner outcomes of education: we teach them that the subjective self is unvalued and even unreal. Their cynicism simply proves that when academic culture dismisses inner truth and honors only the external world, students as well as teachers lose heart.

How can we who teach reclaim our hearts, for the sake of our students, ourselves, and educational reform? That simple question challenges the assumption that drives most reform—that meaningful change comes not from the human heart but from factors external to ourselves, from budgets, methodologies, curricula, and institutional restructuring. Deeper still, it challenges the assumptions about reality and power that drive Western culture.

The foundation of any culture lies in the way it answers the question "Where do reality and power reside?" For some cultures the answer is the gods; for some it is nature; for some it is tradition. In our culture, the answer is clear: reality and power reside in the external world of objects and events and in the sciences that study that world, while the inner realm of the heart is a romantic fantasy, an escape from harsh realities, perhaps, but surely not a source of leverage over the "real" world.

We are obsessed with manipulating externals because we believe that they will give us some power over reality and win us some freedom from its constraints. Mesmerized by a technology that seems to have done just that, we dismiss the inward world. We turn every question we face into an objective problem to be solved—and we believe that for every objective problem there is some sort of technical fix. That is why we train doctors to repair the body but not to honor the spirit; clergy to be CEOs but not spiritual guides; teachers to master techniques but not to engage their students' souls.

Yet at this point in history it should be clear that external "fixes" will not come soon enough to sustain the deepest passions of people who care about teaching. Institutions reform slowly, and as long as we wait, depending on "them" to do the job for us—forgetting that institutions are also "us"—we merely postpone reform and continue the slow slide into cynicism that characterizes too many teaching careers.

There is an alternative to waiting: we can reclaim our belief in the power of inwardness to transform our work and our lives. We became teachers because we once believed that ideas and insight are at least as real and powerful as the world that surrounds us. Now we must remind ourselves that inner reality can give us leverage in the realm of objects and events.

We will find such a reminder in the testimony of Václav Havel, poet and man of practical affairs, a leader in the Velvet Revolution that liberated Czechoslovakia from Soviet rule. It was a revolution that succeeded in the face of obstacles considerably more daunting than those stacked against educational reform.

Havel, now president of the Czech Republic, writes about spending years "under a rock" of institutional oppression that was dropped on the Czech people in the Communist coup of 1968. Then he speaks of the inward seed of human consciousness and how it grew into a flower of reform that cracked and crumbled the granite of totalitarianism a mere twenty years later: "The . . . experience I'm talking about has given me one certainty: . . . the salvation of this human world lies nowhere else than in the human heart, in the human power to reflect, in human meekness and in human responsibility. Without a global revolution in . . . human consciousness, nothing will change for the better, and the catastrophe toward which this world is headed . . . will be unavoidable."[4]

Havel helped the Czech people reclaim their hearts by reminding them who they, and all of us, are: not victims of external forces but persons possessed of an inner power that cannot be taken from us, though we can and do give it away.

Remembering ourselves and our power can lead to revolution, but it requires more than recalling a few facts. *Re-membering* involves putting ourselves back together, recovering identity and integrity, reclaiming the wholeness of our lives. When we forget who we are we do not merely drop some data. We *dis-member* ourselves, with unhappy consequences for our politics, our work, our hearts.

Academics often suffer the pain of dismemberment. On the surface, this is the pain of people who thought they were joining a community of scholars but find themselves in distant, competitive, and uncaring relationships with colleagues and students. Deeper down, this pain is more spiritual than sociological: it comes from being disconnected from our own truth, from the passions that took us into teaching, from the heart that is the source of all good work.

If we have lost the heart to teach, how can we take heart again? How can we re-member who we are, for our own sake and the sake of those we serve?

Mentors Who Evoked Us

If identity and integrity are found at the intersection of the forces that converge in our lives, revisiting some of the convergences that called us toward teaching may allow us to reclaim the selfhood from which good teaching comes. In this section and the next, I want to reflect on two such encounters—with the mentors who evoked us and with the subjects of study that chose us.

The power of our mentors is not necessarily in the models of good teaching they gave us, models that may turn out to have little to do with who we are as teachers. Their power is in their capacity to awaken a truth within us, a truth we can reclaim years later by re-calling their impact on our lives. If we discovered a teacher's heart in ourselves by meeting a great teacher, recalling that meeting may help us take heart in teaching once more.

In faculty workshops, I often ask people to introduce themselves by talking about a teacher who made a difference in their lives. As these stories are told, we are reminded of many facts about good teaching: that it comes in many forms, that the imprint of good teach-ers remains long after the facts they gave us have faded, and that it is important to thank our mentors, no matter how belatedly—partly be-cause we owe them gratitude and partly as a cosmic counterpoint to the apparent ingratitude of our own students!

Then I ask the question that opens to the deeper purpose of this exercise: not "What made your mentor great?" but "What was it about *you* that allowed great mentoring to happen?" Mentoring is a mutuality that requires more than meeting the right teacher: the teacher must meet the right student. In this encounter, not only are the qualities of the mentor revealed, but the qualities of the student are drawn out in a way that is equally revealing.

One of my most memorable mentors was a man who seemed to break every "rule" of good teaching. He lectured at such length, and with such enthusiasm, that he left little room for questions and comments. Preoccupied with the world of thought, he listened poorly to students, not because he disdained them but because he was so eager to teach them by the only way he knew—sharing his knowledge and passions. His classes were mostly monologues, and his students rarely played any role other than audience.

He may sound like a pedagogical nightmare, but for reasons I could not articulate at the time, I was powerfully drawn to his teaching—indeed, he changed my life. Only years later did I understand my attraction and in that understanding are some clues to my identity.

I was the first in my family to attend college. My family valued education, but it offered no exemplars of the intellectual life that has turned out to be my birthright gift. I kept that gift sealed in the box it came in all the way through high school, graduating somewhere below the median of my class, with a major in extracurricular activities. Not until the second semester of college did I open the box, get excited about what was in it, and start doing well at schoolwork, going on to graduate school and into an academic career.

My loquacious professor in college gave me a first glimpse into this part of myself. My excitement in listening to him lay less in what he said—though his ideas were exhilarating—than in discovering a dormant dimension of my identity. It did not matter to me that he violated most rules of good group process and even some rules of considerate personal relations. What mattered was that he generously opened the life of his mind to me, giving full voice to the gift of thought. Something in me knew that this gift was mine as well, though it was years before I could fully trust that knowledge.

Long into my career I harbored a secret sense that thinking and reading and writing, as much as I loved them, did not qualify as "real work." I taught and wrote, but I "justified" myself by working as an administrator for various institutions and projects—work that was practical and thus worthy, like that done by honored members of my family. Only in my mid-forties was I finally able to claim the life of the mind as the mainstay of my vocation, to trust the calling of my soul, a trust that deepened when I was able to decode this early experience of being mentored.

As we recall our mentors, not all of our self-insights are as happy as the one I have just drawn. We sometimes take the wrong lessons from the mentors who draw us when we are young and impressionable.

I witnessed such a case at a faculty workshop I led a few years ago. My on-campus host had taken pains to warn me about Professor X, a curmudgeonly and unpopular teacher, though brilliant in his scholarly field. Of the forty people in the workshop, my host said, Professor X had probably signed up not to learn about teaching but to debunk what we were doing.

In trepidation, I began the workshop with something "soft," inviting people to introduce themselves by talking about their mentors. By the time we got to Professor X, six or eight people had spoken, many with insight and feeling, and a spirit of openness filled the room. I tensed as he began to speak, fearing that this spirit was about to be killed. But it soon became clear that he, too, had been touched by the quality of the exchange.

He told the story of his mentor with the hesitancy that comes from speaking of sacred things and—as he talked about how hard he had tried to model his own career after his mentor's—he surprised us, and surely himself, by choking up.

Later, in private conversation with him, I learned the reason for his emotions. For twenty years, Professor X had tried to imitate his mentor's way of teaching and being, and it had been a disaster. He and his mentor were very different people, and X's attempt to clone his mentor's style had distorted his own identity and integrity. He had lost himself in an identity not his own—a painful insight that took courage to embrace, but one with the promise of growth.

Professor X's story gave me some insight into myself, an example of the mutual illumination that often occurs when we are willing to explore our inner dynamics with each other. Early in my career, I, too, had tried to emulate my mentor with nonstop lecturing, until I realized that my students were even less enthralled by my cheap imitation than some of my classmates had been by the genuine original.

I began to look for a way to teach that was more integral to my own nature, a way that would have as much integrity for me as my mentor's had for him—for the key to my mentor's power was the coherence between his method and himself. I began the long process of trying to understand my own nature as a teacher and to learn the techniques that might help it along.

Though I need sometimes to lecture and may even enjoy doing it, lecturing all the time simply bores me: I usually know what I am going to say, and I have heard it all before. But dialogical methods of teaching help keep me alive. Forced to listen, respond, and improvise, I am more likely to hear something unexpected and insightful from myself as well as others.

That does not mean that lecturing is the wrong way to teach. It simply means that my identity, unlike my mentor's, is more fulfilled in dialogue. When I was young and did not know who I was, I needed someone to model the intellectual gift that might be mine. But now, in midlife, knowing myself better, my identity demands that I use my gift in interaction and interdependence with others.

Here, I believe, is the proper and powerful role of technique: *as we learn more about who we are, we can learn techniques that reveal rather than conceal the personhood from which good teaching comes.* We no longer need to use technique to mask the subjective self, as the culture of professionalism encourages us to do. Now we can use technique to manifest more fully the gift of self from which our best teaching comes.

The self-knowledge that comes from these reflections is crucial to my teaching, for it reveals a complexity within me that is within my students as well. In my case, the "I" who teaches is both intimidated by and attracted to the life of the mind; for a long time it was bedeviled by a sense that the intellectual work it felt called to do was nonetheless a fraud. This "I," despite its intrigue with ideas, was once so unsure of itself that it welcomed a mentor whose performance barred participation. But today, this same "I" finds its own performance boring and needs to be nurtured in dialogue.

When I forget my own inner multiplicity and my own long and continuing journey toward selfhood, my expectations of students become excessive and unreal. If I can remember the inner pluralism of my own soul and the slow pace of my own self-emergence, I will be better able to serve the pluralism among my students at the pace of their young lives. By remembering our mentors, we remember ourselves—and by remembering ourselves, we remember our students.

Looking back, I realize that I was blessed with mentors at every crucial stage of my young life, at every point where my identity needed to grow: in adolescence, in college, in graduate school, and early in my professional career. But a funny thing happened on the way to full adulthood: the mentors stopped coming. For several years I waited for the next one in vain, and for several years my own growth was on hold.

Then I realized what was happening. I was no longer an apprentice, so I no longer needed mentors. It was my turn to become a mentor to someone else. I needed to turn around and look for the new life emerging behind me, to offer to younger people the gift that had been given to me when I was young. As I did, my identity and integrity had new chances to evolve in each new encounter with my students' lives.

Mentors and apprentices are partners in an ancient human dance, and one of teaching's great rewards is the daily chance it gives us to get back on the dance floor. It is the dance of the spiraling generations, in which the old empower the young with their experience and the young empower the old with new life, reweaving the fabric of the human community as they touch and turn.

SUBJECTS THAT CHOSE US

Many of us were called to teach by encountering not only a mentor but also a particular field of study. We were drawn to a body of knowledge because it shed light on our identity as well as on the world. We did not merely find a subject to teach—the subject also found us. We may recover the heart to teach by remembering how that subject evoked a sense of self that was only dormant in us before we encountered the subject's way of naming and framing life.

Alice Kaplan is a teacher of French language and literature, and she has done this kind of remembering in a book called *French Lessons*. "Why do people want to adopt another culture?" she asks as she summarizes her journey into teaching and into life. "Because there's something in their own they don't like, that doesn't *name* them."[5] French culture gave Kaplan a way of claiming an identity and integrity she could not find in the culture to which she was born.

Recalling a course she taught in which a bigoted young man learned to appreciate the stranger through encountering another people in another language, Kaplan reflects: "Moments like this make me think that speaking a foreign language is . . . a chance for growth, for freedom, for liberation from the ugliness of our received ideas and mentalities."[6]

But Kaplan also understands the shadow side of a borrowed identity: "Learning French did me some harm by giving me a place to hide. If life got too messy, I could take off into my second world." But, she says, "writing about it has made me air my suspicions, my anger, my longings, to people for whom it's come as a total surprise."[7] The self-knowledge she gained by asking why she was attracted to her field helped her reconnect, wrestle with, and even redeem troubling events and relationships in her life, renewing her teacher's heart.

Reading Kaplan's reflections (richer by far in shadow and light than my brief review suggests), I was encouraged to make my own. My undergraduate majors were philosophy and sociology, and many of the details I once knew about those fields have long since leached away. But I still recall, thirty-five years later, the moment I discovered C. Wright Mills's idea of the "sociological imagination."[8] I was not merely taken with it—I was possessed by it.

The essence of his idea is simple, but it was radical to me: we cannot see what is "out there" merely by looking around. Everything depends on the lenses through which we view the world. By putting on new lenses, we can see things that would otherwise remain invisible.

Mills taught me how to view the world through the lenses of social theory, and when I took my first look, the world jumped out at me as if I had donned the 3-D movie glasses that Hollywood was hawking at the time. I saw the invisible structures and secret signals that shape our social lives, that have a power over us that I thought resided only in face-to-face relationships. I was astonished at this new vision of life in which people walked about, not freely, as I had imagined, but controlled by strings attached to their minds and hearts by invisible puppeteers.

Why was I so deeply drawn to the idea of the sociological imagination? Why did it become such a defining feature of my worldview? By reflecting on those questions, I have re-membered some key features of who I am.

THE COURAGE TO TEACH

Intellectually, the idea of the sociological imagination spoke to me because at age eighteen I had begun to understand that what you see is not necessarily what you get. I was a child of the 1950s, with its many social fictions, so it took time for me to see that the visible performance of individuals and groups was only the "on-stage" aspect of things, that reality has "backstage" dynamics far more influential than the performance we see up front.

But my attraction to Mills's concept was more than intellectual—it helped me come to terms with some of my deepest personal fears. As a young person, I found the on-stage world both seductive and intimidating. It was an arena of visibility where I wanted to perform and become known, but also an arena where my competence would be tested and surely found wanting. As I came to understand the backstage realities revealed by the sociological imagination, I was able to shake off some of my performance fears.

By looking backstage and seeing how human, how klutzy, how ordinary the mechanics of performance really are—how unlike the glitz and glamour of on-stage performance itself—I could ask myself, "If they can do it, why not me?" This backstage knowledge gave me the comfort of knowing that all heroes have feet of clay; it had the calming effect of the counsel given to nervous public speakers, "Imagine your audience naked."

But my attraction to the sociological imagination went deeper still—beyond intellectual interest, beyond performance fears, to a gap within my own soul. Mills's distinction between the on-stage show and backstage reality mirrored a great divide in my inner life. Outwardly, I had learned how to make my performance seem relatively smooth and accomplished, but inwardly, I felt anxious and fumbling and inept.

The constant contradiction between how I experienced myself and how other people viewed me created a painful, sometimes crippling sense of fraudulence. But the sociological imagination and its view of societal duplicity helped me understand how common that contradiction is, how basic to the human condition, and my sense of fraudulence became less onerous.

It has taken me a long time to turn Mills's insight from an analysis of our society toward an understanding of myself. The sociological imagination is easily used as one of those "debunking" tools, beloved of social science, that allows us to stand detached by the side of the road as the parade passes by, sniping at its silliness and pretending to be above it all.

For a long time, I stood off to the side as critic and judge, and now I understand why: I was projecting onto society all the fraudulence I felt but could not face in myself, and I was using that projection as a way of evading my own dividedness. I no longer want to live that way—which is why I take pains in my writing to counterbalance the truth of the sociological imagination.

Earlier in this chapter, I insisted that our inner world has a reality and a power that can keep us from being victims of circumstance and compel us to take responsibility for our own lives. In effect, I argued that the world of social structures and signals need not dictate our lives, that the sociological imagination that so entranced me as a young man (and has its grip on me yet) does not hold all the answers. In the very act of writing this chapter, I have been encountering my subject—and myself—anew, still respectful of the power of social facts but unwilling to use that knowledge as an escape from personal responsibility.

What I have learned about my identity as a teacher from this re-membering is, to some extent, encouraging: I would not be an advocate of the power of inner reality if I had not reached some degree of congruence between my on-stage and backstage lives.

But I have also learned that my conflict between on-stage and backstage reality is far from being resolved—it continues to come up in my teaching. That conflict was the theme of the teaching stories I told at the start of this chapter, stories whose drama, such as it is, lies in the tension between my external response to classroom events and my internal sense of incompetence.

One of my favorite essays on teaching is Jane Tompkins's "Pedagogy of the Distressed."[9] It seems to have been written directly to my divided condition. With wonderful candor, Tompkins says that her obsession as a teacher had not been with helping students learn what they wanted and needed to know but rather with "(a) showing the students how smart I was; (b) showing them how knowledgeable I was; and (c) showing them how well prepared I was for class. I had been putting on a performance whose true goal was not to help the

THE COURAGE TO TEACH

students learn but to act in such a way that they would have a good opinion of me."

Then she asks, "How did it come to be that our main goal as academicians turned out to be performance?" Her answer rings true to me—fear: "Fear of being shown up for what you are: a fraud, stupid, ignorant, a clod, a dolt, a sap, a weakling, someone who can't cut the mustard."

That is how it sometimes is for me. Driven by fear that my backstage ineptitude will be exposed, I strive to make my on-stage performance slicker and smoother—and in the process, make it less and less likely that my students will learn anything other than how to cover up and show off. I conceal my own heart and am unable to weave the fabric of connectedness that teaching and learning require.

Once again: when I seek my identity and integrity, what I find is not always a proud and shining thing. The discoveries I make about myself when I remember the encounters that have shaped and revealed my selfhood are sometimes embarrassing—but they are also real. Whatever the cost in embarrassment, I will know myself better, and thus be a better teacher, when I acknowledge the forces at play within me instead of allowing them to wreak witless havoc on my work.

Florida Scott-Maxwell, writing in her mid-eighties, made the point powerfully: "You need only claim the events of your life to make yourself yours. When you truly possess all you have been and done . . . you are fierce with reality."[10]

THE TEACHER WITHIN

Encounters with mentors and subjects can awaken a sense of self and yield clues to who we are. But the call to teach does not come from external encounters alone—no outward teacher or teaching will have much effect until my soul assents. Any authentic call ultimately comes from the voice of the *teacher within,* the voice that invites me to honor the nature of my true self.

By the voice of the inward teacher, I do not mean *conscience* or *superego,* moral arbiter or internalized judge. In fact, conscience, as it is commonly understood, can get us into deep vocational trouble.

The Heart of a Teacher

When we listen primarily for what we "ought" to be doing with our lives, we may find ourselves hounded by external expectations that can distort our identity and integrity. There is much that I ought to be doing by some abstract moral calculus. But is it my vocation? Am I gifted and called to do it? Is this particular ought a place of intersection between my inner self and the outer world, or is it someone else's image of how my life should look?

When I follow only the oughts, I may find myself doing work that is ethically laudable but not mine to do. A vocation that is not mine, no matter how externally valued, does violence to the self—in the precise sense that it *violates* my identity and integrity on behalf of some abstract norm. When I violate myself, I invariably end up violating the people I work with. How many teachers inflict their own pain on their students, the pain that comes from doing what never was, or no longer is, their true work?

In contrast to the strained and even violent concept of vocation as an ought, Frederick Buechner offers a more generous and humane image of vocation as "the place where your deep gladness and the world's deep hunger meet."[11]

In a culture that sometimes equates work with suffering, it is revolutionary to suggest that the best inward sign of vocation is deep gladness—revolutionary but true. If a work is mine to do, it will make me glad over the long haul, despite the difficult days. Even the difficult days will ultimately gladden me, because they pose the kinds of problems that can help me grow in a work if it is truly mine.

If a work does not gladden me in these ways, I need to consider laying it down. When I devote myself to something that does not flow from my identity, that is not integral to my nature, I am most likely deepening the world's hunger rather than helping to alleviate it.

There are times when we must work for money rather than meaning, and we may never have the luxury of quitting a job because it does not make us glad. But that does not release us from continually checking the violence we do to others and ourselves by working in ways that violate our souls. Nor does it relieve us from wondering whether preserving integrity is a luxury. What brings more security in the long run: holding this job or honoring my soul?

The teacher within is not the voice of conscience but of identity and integrity. It speaks not of what ought to be but of what is real for us, of what is true. It says things like, "This is what fits you and this is what doesn't"; "This is who you are and this is who you are not"; "This is what gives you life and this is what kills your spirit—or makes you wish you were dead." The teacher within stands guard at the gate of selfhood, warding off whatever insults our integrity and welcoming whatever affirms it. The voice of the inward teacher reminds me of my truth as I negotiate the force field of my life.

I realize that the idea of a teacher within strikes some academics as a romantic fantasy, but I cannot fathom why. If there is no such reality in our lives, centuries of Western discourse about the aims of education become so much lip-flapping. In classical understanding, education is the attempt to "lead out" from within the self a core of wisdom that has the power to resist falsehood and live in the light of truth, not by external norms but by reasoned and reflective self-determination. The inward teacher is the living core of our lives that is addressed and evoked by any education worthy of the name.

Perhaps the idea is unpopular because it compels us to look at two of the most difficult truths about teaching. The first is that what we teach will never "take" unless it connects with the inward, living core of our students' lives, with our students' inward teachers.

We can, and do, make education an exclusively outward enterprise, forcing students to memorize and repeat facts without ever appealing to their inner truth—and we get predictable results: many students never want to read a challenging book or think a creative thought once they get out of school. The kind of teaching that transforms people does not happen if the student's inward teacher is ignored.

The second truth is even more daunting: we can speak to the teacher within our students only when we are on speaking terms with the teacher within ourselves.

The student who said that her bad teachers spoke like cartoon characters was describing teachers who have grown deaf to their inner guide, who have so thoroughly separated inner truth from outer actions that they have lost touch with a sense of self. Deep speaks to deep, and when we have not sounded our own depths, we cannot sound the depths of our students' lives.

How does one attend to the voice of the teacher within? I have no particular methods to suggest, other than the familiar ones: solitude and silence, meditative reading and walking in the woods, keeping a journal, finding a friend who will listen. I simply propose that we need to learn as many ways as we can of "talking to ourselves."

That phrase, of course, is one we normally use to name a symptom of mental imbalance—a clear sign of how our culture regards the idea of an inner voice! But people who learn to talk to themselves may soon delight in the discovery that the teacher within is the sanest conversation partner they have ever had.

We need to find every possible way to listen to that voice and take its counsel seriously, not only for the sake of our work but for the sake of our own health as well. If someone in the outer world is trying to tell us something important and we ignore his or her presence, the person either gives up and stops speaking or becomes more and more violent in attempting to get our attention.

Similarly, if we do not respond to the voice of the inward teacher, it will either stop speaking or become violent: I am convinced that some forms of depression, of which I have personal experience, are induced by a long-ignored inner teacher trying desperately to get us to listen by threatening to destroy us. When we honor that voice with simple attention, it responds by speaking more gently and engaging us in a life-giving conversation of the soul.

That conversation does not have to reach conclusions to be of value: we do not need to emerge from talking to ourselves with clear goals, objectives, and plans. Measuring the value of inner dialogue by its practical outcomes is like measuring the value of a friendship by the number of problems that are solved when friends get together.

Conversation among friends has its own rewards: in the presence of our friends, we have the simple joy of feeling at ease, at home, trusted and able to trust. We attend to the inner teacher not to get fixed but to befriend the deeper self, to cultivate a sense of identity and integrity that allows us to feel at home wherever we are.

Listening to the inner teacher also offers an answer to one of the most basic questions teachers face: How can I develop the *authority* to teach, the capacity to stand my ground in the midst of the complex forces of both the classroom and my own life?

In a culture of technique, we often confuse authority with power, but the two are not the same. Power works from the outside in, but authority works from the inside out. We are mistaken when we seek authority outside ourselves, in sources ranging from the subtle skills of group process to that less than subtle method of social control called grading. This view of teaching turns the teacher into the cop on the corner, trying to keep things moving amicably and by consent but always having recourse to the coercive power of the law.

External tools of power have occasional utility in teaching, but they are no substitute for authority, the authority that comes from the teacher's inner life. The clue is in the word itself, which has *author* at its core. Authority is granted to people who are perceived as *authoring* their own words, their own actions, their own lives, rather than playing a scripted role at great remove from their own hearts. When teachers depend on the coercive powers of law or technique, they have no authority at all.

I am painfully aware of the times in my own teaching when I lose touch with my inner teacher and therefore with my own authority. In those times I try to gain power by barricading myself behind the podium and my status while wielding the threat of grades. But when my teaching is authorized by the teacher within me, I need neither weapons nor armor to teach.

Authority comes as I reclaim my identity and integrity, remembering my selfhood and my sense of vocation. Then teaching can come from the depths of my own truth—and the truth that is within my students has a chance to respond in kind.

Chapter II

A Culture of Fear

Education and the Disconnected Life

Day after day up there beating my wings
with all of the softness truth requires
I feel them shrug whenever I pause:
they class my voice among tentative things,

And they credit fact, force, battering.
I dance my way toward the family of knowing,
embracing stray error as a long-lost boy
and bringing him home with my fluttering.

Every quick feather asserts a just claim;
it bites like a saw into white pine.
I communicate right; but explain to the dean—
well, Right has a long and intricate name.

And the saying of it is a lonely thing.

—WILLIAM STAFFORD, "LIT INSTRUCTOR"[1]

AN ANATOMY OF FEAR

If we want to develop and deepen the capacity for connectedness at the heart of good teaching, we must understand—and resist—the perverse but powerful draw of the "disconnected" life. How, and why, does academic culture discourage us from living connected lives? How, and why, does it encourage us to distance ourselves from our students and our subjects, to teach and learn at some remove from our own hearts?

On the surface, the answer seems obvious: we are distanced by a grading system that separates teachers from students, by departments that fragment fields of knowledge, by competition that makes students and teachers alike wary of their peers, and by a bureaucracy that puts faculty and administration at odds.

Educational institutions are full of divisive structures, of course, but blaming them for our brokenness perpetuates the myth that the outer world is more powerful than the inner. The external structures of education would not have the power to divide us as deeply as they do if they were not rooted in one of the most compelling features of our inner landscape—fear.

If we withdrew our assent from these structures, they would collapse, an academic version of the Velvet Revolution. But we collaborate with them, fretting from time to time about their "reform," because they so successfully exploit our fear. Fear is what distances us from our colleagues, our students, our subjects, ourselves. Fear shuts down those "experiments with truth" that allow us to weave a wider web of connectedness—and thus shuts down our capacity to teach as well.

From grade school on, education is a fearful enterprise. As a student, I was in too many classrooms riddled with fear, the fear that leads many children, born with a love of learning, to hate the idea of school. As a teacher, I am at my worst when fear takes the lead in me, whether that means teaching in fear of my students or manipulating their fears of me. Our relations as faculty colleagues are often diminished by fear; fear is nearly universal in the relations of faculty and administration; and fear is a standard management tool in too many administrative kit bags.

After thirty years of teaching, my own fear remains close at hand. It is there when I enter a classroom and feel the undertow into which I have jumped. It is there when I ask a question—and my students keep a silence as stony as if I had asked them to betray their friends. It is there whenever it feels as if I have lost control: a mind-boggling question is asked, an irrational conflict emerges, or students get lost in my lecture because I myself am lost. When a class that has gone badly comes to a merciful end, I am fearful long after it is over—fearful that I am not just a bad teacher but a bad person, so closely is my sense of self tied to the work I do.

My own fear is matched by the fear within my students, though in my early years of teaching I conveniently forgot that fact. From where I stood, exposed and vulnerable at the front of the room, my students seemed enviously safe, hidden behind their notebooks, anonymous in the midst of the crowd.

I should have remembered from my own experience that students, too, are afraid: afraid of failing, of not understanding, of being drawn into issues they would rather avoid, of having their ignorance exposed or their prejudices challenged, of looking foolish in front of their peers. When my students' fears mix with mine, fear multiplies geometrically—and education is paralyzed.

If we were to turn some of our externalized reformist energies toward exorcising the inner demons of fear, we would take a vital step toward the renewal of teaching and learning. We would no longer need to put our lives on hold while waiting for structural change. By understanding our fear, we could overcome the structures of disconnection with the power of self-knowledge.

What is the fear that keeps us beholden to those structures? Again, the answer seems obvious: it is the fear of losing my job or my image or my status if I do not pay homage to institutional powers. But that explanation does not go deep enough.

We collaborate with the structures of separation because they promise to protect us against one of the deepest fears at the heart of being human—the fear of having a live encounter with alien "otherness," whether the other is a student, a colleague, a subject, or a self-dissenting voice within. We fear encounters in which the other is free to be itself, to speak its own truth, to tell us what we may not wish to hear. We want those encounters on our own terms, so that we can control their outcomes, so that they will not threaten our view of world and self.

Academic institutions offer myriad ways to protect ourselves from the threat of a live encounter. To avoid a live encounter with teachers, students can hide behind their notebooks and their silence. To avoid a live encounter with students, teachers can hide behind their podiums, their credentials, their power. To avoid a live encounter with one another, faculty can hide behind their academic specialties.

To avoid a live encounter with subjects of study, teachers and students alike can hide behind the pretense of objectivity: students can say, "Don't ask me to think about this stuff—just give me the facts," and faculty can say, "Here are the facts—don't think about them, just get them straight." To avoid a live encounter with ourselves, we can learn the art of self-alienation, of living a divided life.

This fear of the live encounter is actually a sequence of fears that begins in the fear of diversity. As long as we inhabit a universe made homogeneous by our refusal to admit otherness, we can maintain the illusion that we possess the truth about ourselves and the world—after all, there is no "other" to challenge us! But as soon as we admit pluralism, we are forced to admit that ours is not the only standpoint, the only experience, the only way, and the truths we have built our lives on begin to feel fragile.

If we embrace diversity, we find ourselves on the doorstep of our next fear: fear of the conflict that will ensue when divergent truths meet. Because academic culture knows only one form of conflict, the win-lose form called competition, we fear the live encounter as a contest from which one party emerges victorious while the other leaves defeated and ashamed. To evade public engagement over our dangerous differences, we privatize them, only to find them growing larger and more divisive.

If we peel back our fear of conflict, we find a third layer of fear, the fear of losing identity. Many of us are so deeply identified with our ideas that when we have a competitive encounter, we risk losing more than the debate: we risk losing our sense of self.

Of course, there are forms of conflict more creative than the win-lose form called competition, forms that are vital if the self is to grow. But academic culture knows little of these alternative forms—such as consensual decision making—in which all can win and none need lose, in which "winning" means emerging from the encounter with a larger sense of self than one brought into it, in which we learn that the self is not a scrap of turf to be defended but a capacity to be enlarged.

If we embrace the promise of diversity, of creative conflict, and of "losing" in order to "win," we still face one final fear—the fear that a live encounter with otherness will challenge or even compel us to change our lives. This is not paranoia: the world really is out to get us! Otherness, taken seriously, always invites transformation, calling us not only to new facts and theories and values but also to new ways of living our lives—and that is the most daunting threat of all.

Our multilayered fear of the live encounter is not simply a personal emotion that teachers and students bring into the classroom one by one. It is also a cultural trait at work in every area of our common life. We practice a politics of fear in which candidates are elected by playing on voters' anxieties about race and class. We do business in an economy of fear where "getting and spending" are driven by consumer worries about keeping up with the neighbors. We subscribe to religions of fear that exploit our dread of death and damnation. In a culture where fear is the air we breathe, it is hard to see how deeply fearful our education is—let alone imagine another way to teach and learn.

This chapter focuses on pathological fear, so it is important to remember that fear can also be healthy. Some fears can help us survive, even learn and grow—if we know how to decode them. My fear that I am teaching poorly may be not a sign of failure but evidence that I care about my craft. My fear that a topic will explode in the classroom may be not a warning to flee from it but a signal that the topic must be addressed. My fear of teaching at the dangerous intersection of the personal and the public may be not cowardice but confirmation that I am taking the risks that good teaching requires.

Fear can also play a positive role in students' lives. When Albert Camus writes, "What gives value to travel is fear," his words could easily apply to the forays that good teachers make with their students across landscapes of alien truth.[2] Camus speaks of the fear we feel when we encounter something foreign and are challenged to enlarge our thinking, our identity, our lives—the fear that lets us know we are on the brink of real learning: "It is the fact that, at a certain moment, when we are so far from our own country . . . we are seized by a vague fear, and an instinctive desire to go back to the protection of old habits. . . . At that moment, we are feverish but also porous, so that the slightest touch makes us quiver to the depths of our being. We come across a cascade of light, and there is eternity."[3]

The fear that makes people "porous" to real learning is a healthy fear that enhances education, and we must find ways to encourage it. But first we must deal with the fear that makes us not porous but impervious, that shuts down our capacity for connectedness and destroys our ability to teach and learn.

I want to examine three places where that shutdown occurs: in the lives of our students, in our own self-protective hearts, and in our dominant way of knowing. We will be freed from these pathologies neither by technique nor by structural reform but rather by insight into how and why fear dominates our lives.

THE STUDENT FROM HELL

The fear that shuts down the capacity for connectedness is often at work in our students. If we could see that fact clearly and consistently—and learn to address our students' fears rather than exploit them—we would move toward better teaching. But seeing is never simple, and the lenses through which many teachers view the young these days tend to distort who, and how, our students really are.

When I ask teachers to name the biggest obstacle to good teaching, the answer I most often hear is "my students." When I ask why this is so, I hear a litany of complaints: my students are silent, sullen, withdrawn; they have little capacity for conversation; they have short attention spans; they do not engage well with ideas; they cling to narrow notions of "relevance" and "usefulness" and dismiss the world of ideas.

If my report seems exaggerated, here is the banner from a recent brochure announcing a national conference on teaching and learning:

IT'S A FACT
Many students have no direction and lack motivation.
These students have little knowledge of the social skills necessary for teamwork and negotiation.
They're bored and passive in situations calling for action, and belligerent and destructive in contexts requiring reflection.

When I inquire about the causes of these alleged faults, I hear another standard litany, this time one of societal ills. Absentee parents and the vanishing family, the deficiencies of public education, the banality of television and mass culture, the ravages of drugs and alcohol—all are held to blame for the diminished state of our students' minds and lives.

As impressive as this list is, the ferocity with which some faculty insist that today's students are vastly inferior to those of their own generation makes one wonder whether social change alone can account for such dramatic decline. Perhaps the DNA itself has degenerated within the past quarter century!

Whatever tidbits of truth these student stereotypes contain, they grossly distort reality, and they widen the disconnection between students and their teachers. Not only do these caricatures make our lives look noble in comparison to the barbaric young, but they also place the sources of our students' problems far upstream from the place where our lives converge with theirs. Criticizing the client is the conventional defense in any embattled profession, and these stereotypes conveniently relieve us of any responsibility for our students' problems—or their resolution.

Some years ago, I met the dean of an experimental college who was guiding that project into its second year on the campus of a major university. He had just come from a faculty meeting, and it was clear from his demeanor that things had not gone well.

"What happened?" I asked.

"The faculty spent most of the morning complaining about the quality of our students. They said that this program would never work if we did not recruit young people who were better prepared."

"What did you tell them?"

"I listened as long as I could," he said, "but they could not get off their blame-the-student shtick. Finally I said that they sounded like doctors in a hospital saying, 'Don't send us any more sick people—we don't know what to do with them. Send us healthy patients so we can look like good doctors.'"

His analogy helped me understand something crucial about teaching: *the way we diagnose our students' condition will determine the kind of remedy we offer.* But we teachers spend little time thinking with each other about the condition of our students, about the maladies for which our teaching is supposed to be the cure. We have nothing to compare with the "grand rounds" common in hospitals, where doctors, nurses, therapists, and other professionals collaborate in diagnosing a patient's need. Instead, we allow our "treatment mode" to be shaped by the thoughtless stereotypes of students that float freely in faculty culture.

The dominant diagnosis, to put it bluntly, is that our "patients" are brain-dead. Small wonder, then, that the dominant treatment is to drip data bits into our students' veins, wheeling their comatose forms from one information source to the next until the prescribed course of treatment is complete, hoping they will absorb enough intellectual nutrients to maintain their vital signs until they have graduated—and paid their tuition in full.

That caricature highlights a truth: our assumption that students are brain-dead leads to pedagogies that deaden their brains. When we teach by dripping information into their passive forms, students who arrive in the classroom alive and well become passive consumers of knowledge and are dead on departure when they graduate. But the power of this self-fulfilling prophecy seems to elude us: we rarely consider that our students may die in the classroom because we use methods that assume they are dead.

I once led a faculty workshop where the conversation had turned toward students, and many participants were complaining about how silent and indifferent they are. The workshop was being held in a glass-walled conference room at the core of a new classroom building, and the curtains that might have shut off our view of the surrounding hallways had been left open. In the midst of the student-bashing, a bell rang and the classrooms surrounding the conference room began to empty out. The halls quickly filled with young people, talking to each other with great energy and animation.

I asked the faculty to observe the evidence before us and then asked them to explain the difference between the students they had been describing and the ones we were now seeing: "Is it possible that your students are not brain-dead? Is it possible that their classroom coma is induced by classroom conditions and that once they cross the threshold into another world, they return to life?"

We need a new diagnosis of our students' inward condition, one that is more perceptive about their needs, less defensive about our own role in their plight, and more likely to lead to creative modes of teaching. I want to suggest such a diagnosis by telling another teaching story from my own experience.

I had just finished a two-day faculty workshop on a Midwestern university campus. Amid high praise for the work we had done together—which, I was told, had given people deeper insight into the pedagogical arts—I was ushered into a political science class where I had agreed to be "teacher for an hour."

I should have left while the leaving was good.

There were thirty students in that classroom. It is possible that twenty-nine of them were ready to learn, but I will never know. For in the back row, in the far corner, slouched the specter called the Student from Hell.

The Student from Hell is a universal archetype that can take male or female form; mine happened to be male. His cap was pulled down over his eyes so that I could not tell whether they were open or shut. His notebooks and writing instruments were nowhere to be seen. It was a fine spring day, but his jacket was buttoned tight, signifying readiness to bolt at any moment.

What I remember most vividly is his posture. Though he sat in one of those sadistic classroom chairs with a rigidly attached desk, he had achieved a position that I know to be anatomically impossible: despite the interposed desk, his body was parallel to the floor. Seeking desperately to find even one redeeming feature in the specter before me, I seized on the idea that he must practice the discipline of hatha yoga to be able to distort his body so completely.

At that point in my life, I had been teaching for twenty-five years. Yet faced with the Student from Hell, I committed the most basic mistake of the greenest neophyte: I became totally obsessed with him, and everyone else in the room disappeared from my screen.

For a long and anguished hour I aimed everything I had at this young man, trying desperately to awaken him from his dogmatic slumbers, but the harder I tried, the more he seemed to recede. Meanwhile, the other students became ciphers as my obsession with the Student from Hell made me oblivious to their needs. I learned that day what a black hole is: a place where the gravity is so intense that all traces of light disappear.

I left that class with a powerful combination of feelings: self-pity, fraudulence, and rage. On the heels of a highly touted workshop on teaching, I had put on a stunningly inept demonstration of the art. The regular teacher had taken my presence as an excuse to skip his own class, so my travesty had gone unobserved by any peer, as usual. But my self-respect was gravely wounded, and I knew whom to blame: it was the fault of the Student from Hell. Self-pity and projected blame—the recipe for a well-lived life!

I was desperate to get out of town, but I had to suffer through one more event, dinner with a few faculty at the president's house. There, the workshop received fresh praise, but now the praise was painful, driving me deeper into feelings of fraudulence. When the president announced the arrival of the college van that would haul me to the airport, I was flooded with relief.

I went out to the driveway, tossed my bags into the back seat of the van, climbed into the front seat, and turned to greet the driver.

It was the Student from Hell.

I am a religious person, so I commenced to pray: "I have sinned, I do sin, and given attractive opportunity, I will probably sin again. But nothing I have ever done or plan to do merits this punishment—an hour and a half in a van with the Student from Hell."

We backed out of the driveway and wound our way through the neighborhood, staring ahead in silence. When we reached the freeway, the driver suddenly spoke: "Dr. Palmer, is it OK if we talk?"

Every atom in my body screamed "No!" But my mouth, which was trained in the suburbs, said, "Sure, fine, yes, you bet."

I will always remember the conversation that followed. The student's father was an unemployed laborer and an alcoholic who thought that his son's desire to finish college and become some sort of professional was utter nonsense.

The young man lived with his father, who berated him daily for his foolishness: "The world is out to get people like us, and college is part of the scam. Drop out, get a fast-food job, save whatever you can, and settle for it. That's how it's always been, and that's how it'll always be."

Daily this young man felt his motivation for college fading away. "Have you ever been in a situation like this?" he asked. "What do you think I should do about it?"

We talked until it was time for my plane to take off, and for a while afterward we corresponded. I do not know whether I helped him—but I know that he helped me. He helped me understand that the silent and seemingly sullen students in our classrooms are not brain-dead: they are full of fear.

The Student from Hell is not born that way but is created by conditions beyond his or her control. Yes, one or two of them may have been sent here directly by Satan to destroy Western civilization as we know and love it. But this particular student—whose plight represents many others—forced me into a deeper understanding of the student condition, one that is slowly transforming the way I teach.

Students are marginalized people in our society. The silence that we face in the classroom is the silence that has always been adopted by people on the margin—people who have reason to fear those in power and have learned that there is safety in not speaking.

For years, African Americans were silent in the presence of whites—silent, that is, about their true thoughts and feelings. For years, women were similarly silent in the presence of men. Today all of that is changing as blacks and women move from the margins to the center and speak truths that people like me need to hear.

But young people remain marginalized in our society—and their plight has worsened since the 1960s as we have become more and more fearful and dismissive of our youth. Implicitly and explicitly, young people are told that they have no experience worth having, no voice worth speaking, no future of any note, no significant role to play.

Is it any wonder that students, having received such messages from a dozen sources, stay silent in the classroom rather than risk another dismissal or rebuke? Their silence is born not of stupidity or banality but of a desire to protect themselves and to survive. It is a silence driven by their fear of an adult world in which they feel alien and disempowered.

Of course, some of our students are not young in years. Some have returned to school in midlife and may even be older than their teachers. But the fear in our younger students has its counterpart in our older students as well. Nontraditional students often return to school because of an experience that puts them, too, on the margins— a divorce, the failure of a career, the death of a spouse. We think of them as more expressive and self-confident than their younger peers, but perhaps their years have merely given them more practice at keeping their fears tucked away. Inwardly, these students relate to teachers as "elders," even if the age difference is reversed, and they may easily be as apprehensive about how we will respond to them as younger students tend to be.

If I want to teach well in the face of my students' fears, I need to see clearly and steadily the fear that is in their hearts. No technique could have altered my classroom debacle with the Student from Hell, because the trouble began in a more inward, less tractable place, in my failure to read him and his behavior perceptively. I read that student not in the light of his condition but in the shadow of my own (a point to which I will return shortly), and my self-absorbed misreading led me into one of my lowest moments in teaching.

The behaviors generated by fear—silence, withdrawal, cynicism—often mimic those that come with ignorance, so it is not always easy for me to keep believing, when I look at some of my students, that anxiety rather than banality is what I am looking at. I need to keep renewing my insight into my students' true condition in spite of misleading appearances.

It is not easy, but it is rewarding. As I have come to understand my students' fears, I have been able to aim my teaching in a new direction. I no longer teach to their imputed ignorance, having rejected that assessment as both inaccurate and self-serving. Instead, I try to teach to their fearful hearts, and when I am able to do so, their minds often come along as well.

I now understand what Nelle Morton meant when she said that one of the great tasks in our time is to "hear people to speech."[4] Behind their fearful silence, our students want to find their voices, speak their voices, have their voices heard. A good teacher is one who can listen to those voices even before they are spoken—so that someday they can speak with truth and confidence.

What does it mean to listen to a voice before it is spoken? It means making space for the other, being aware of the other, paying attention to the other, honoring the other. It means not rushing to fill our students' silences with fearful speech of our own and not trying to coerce them into saying the things that we want to hear. It means entering empathetically into the student's world so that he or she perceives you as someone who has the promise of being able to hear another person's truth.

In the story of the Student from Hell there is a powerful image that offers a clue about how to hear students into speech: that young man found his voice when he was literally "behind the wheel." Sitting passively in the classroom while I held forth, he was reduced to silence. But given a real responsibility, put in charge of my schedule and my safety, he found a voice to speak of significant things.

As I find ways to put my students behind the wheel, I will encourage more and more of them to find their voices and speak for themselves. There are methods that can help me do this, and I will explore some of them later in this book. But before I can use those methods with integrity and with effectiveness, I must understand the fear within my students' hearts—and the fear that is in my own.

THE TEACHER'S FEARFUL HEART

Why do we have so much trouble seeing students as they really are? Why do we diagnose their condition in morbid terms that lead to deadly modes of teaching? Why do we not see the fear that is in their hearts and find ways to help them through it, rather than accusing them of being ignorant and banal?

On one level, the answer is simple: our conventional diagnosis allows us to ignore our failings as teachers by blaming the victims. But there is a deeper reason for our blindness to our students' fears, and it is more daunting: we cannot see the fear in our students until we see the fear in ourselves. When we deny our own condition, we resist seeing anything in others that might remind us of who, and how, *we* really are.

If you were reading between the lines in my story of the Student from Hell, you know that there are two morals to that tale. One is about the fear in the student; the other is about the fear within me.

Looked at "objectively," it is hard to believe that I was afraid of that young man—thus demonstrating the limits of objectivity. There I was, at a small university in the Midwest from which I would soon take leave, having gained the approval of the people who had hired me, on whom my livelihood depends. There I was in my early fifties, career in full flight, doing work I find rich in meaning, blessed with health and family and friends. There I was, face to face with a forlorn young man in his early twenties who had no apparent power over me—and I was so afraid of him that I lost my bearings, my capacity to teach, my sense of self and self-worth.

In unguarded moments with close friends, we who teach will acknowledge a variety of fears: having our work go unappreciated, being inadequately rewarded, discovering one fine morning that we chose the wrong profession, spending our lives on trivia, ending up feeling like frauds. But many of us have another fear that we rarely name: our fear of the judgment of the young.

Day after day, year after year, we walk into classrooms and look into younger faces that *seem* to signal, in ways crude and subtle, "You're history. Whatever you value, we don't—and since you couldn't possibly understand the things we value, we won't even bother to try to tell you what they are. We are here only because we are forced to be here. So whatever you have to do, get it over with, and let us get on with our lives."

That is how we sometimes *interpret* the signals our students send when, in truth, they are usually signals of fear, not disdain. Until I learn to decode that message, I will be quick to cast too many of my students in the role of the Student from Hell—and I will never learn to decode it until I understand my own fear of the judgment of the young.

Erik Erikson, reflecting on adult development, says that in midlife we face a choice between "stagnation" and "generativity."[5] Erikson's notion can be useful even if you are a young teacher, once you understand that teachers age at a geometric rate: my best guess is that most teachers reach midlife by the time they turn twenty-nine! When one returns to work each fall and finds one's students the same age they were last year, middle age comes long before its time.

Stagnation is the state chosen by teachers who are so threatened by students that they barricade themselves behind their credentials, their podiums, their status, their research. Ironically, this choice for stagnation mirrors the disengagement of the students these teachers fear. Having been wounded by fearful young people who hold their teachers at arm's length, these teachers fearfully fend off their students, thus feeding the cycle of fear.

It not unusual to see faculty in midcareer don the armor of cynicism against students, education, and any sign of hope. It is the cynicism that comes when the high hopes one once had for teaching have been dashed by experience—or by the failure to interpret one's experience accurately. I am always impressed by the intensity of this cynicism, for behind it I feel the intensity of the hopes that brought these faculty into teaching. Perhaps those hopes can be rekindled, because the intensity is still there: rightly understood, this sort of cynicism may contain the seeds of its own renewal.

The way of renewal, according to Erik Erikson, is called generativity. It is a lovely and exact word because it suggests two related dimensions of a healthy adult identity.

On one hand, it suggests *creativity,* the ongoing possibility that no matter our age, we can help co-create the world. On the other hand, it suggests the endless emergence of the *generations,* with its implied imperative that the elders look back toward the young and help them find a future that the elders will not see. Put these two images together, and generativity becomes "creativity in the service of the young"—a way in which the elders serve not only the young but also their own well-being.

In the face of the apparent judgment of the young, teachers must turn toward students, not away from them, saying, in effect, "There are great gaps between us. But no matter how wide and perilous they may be, I am committed to bridging them—not only because you need me to help you on your way but also because I need your insight and energy to help renew my own life."

I have thought a great deal about my fear of the Student from Hell, and it seems to have two parts. One of them I hope to lose some day, but the other I hope always to have with me.

The fear I want to get rid of is rooted in my need to be popular with young people—a need that may be endemic among people who become teachers but one that keeps us from serving our students well. This fear is pathological. It leads me to pander to students, to lose both my dignity and my way, so worried that the sloucher in the back row doesn't like me that I fail to teach him and everyone else in the room.

But I hope never to lose the other part of my fear—the fear I feel when I am not in life-giving communion with the young. I hope never to encounter an alienated student sitting in the back row of a class and act as if he or she did not exist: when the Student from Hell ceases to be relevant to me, my life becomes less relevant to the world.

Reflecting on my experience with the Student from Hell, I reproach myself for having failed to teach well that day. But it is also true that *something* that I did in that classroom made it possible for that young man to approach me a few hours later about one of the deepest dilemmas of his life. Something I did helped draw that young man into a relationship where he was able to speak his truth.

Perhaps what reached him, despite my fear and my ineptitude, was my yearning for a generative relationship, my yearning "not to be cut off." It is easier to forgive myself for failing the rest of those students when I name what may well be true: that my passion to connect with one student somehow got through to him and eventually empowered him to speak. When he spoke, he addressed not only his own need but my need as well—my need to stay connected with the life of the rising generation.

Good teaching is an act of hospitality toward the young, and hospitality is always an act that benefits the host even more than the guest. The concept of hospitality arose in ancient times when this reciprocity was easier to see: in nomadic cultures, the food and shelter one gave to a stranger yesterday is the food and shelter one hopes to receive from a stranger tomorrow. By offering hospitality, one participates in the endless reweaving of a social fabric on which all can depend—thus the gift of sustenance for the guest becomes a gift of hope for the host. It is that way in teaching as well: the teacher's hospitality to the student results in a world more hospitable to the teacher.

One of the blessings of teaching is the chance it gives us for continuing encounters with the young, but whatever eventually blesses us may at first feel like a curse! We are more likely to survive the curse and arrive at the blessing if we understand that we may be as afraid of our students as they are of us—and then learn to decode our own fears, as well as theirs, for the sake of creativity in the service of the young.

OUR FEARFUL WAY OF KNOWING

The personal fears that students and teachers bring to the classroom are fed by the fact that the roots of education are sunk deep in fearful ground. The ground I have in mind is one we rarely name: it is our dominant mode of knowing, a mode promoted with such arrogance that it is hard to see the fear behind it—until one remembers that arrogance often masks fear.

A mode of knowing arises from the way we answer two questions at the heart of the educational mission: How do we know what we know? And by what warrant can we call our knowledge true? Our answers may be largely tacit, even unconscious, but they are continually communicated in the way we teach and learn.

If we regard truth as something handed down from authorities on high, the classroom will look like a dictatorship. If we regard truth as a fiction determined by personal whim, the classroom will look like anarchy. If we regard truth as emerging from a complex process of mutual inquiry, the classroom will look like a resourceful and interdependent community. Our assumptions about knowing can open up, or shut down, the capacity for connectedness on which good teaching depends.

The mode of knowing that dominates education creates disconnections between teachers, their subjects, and their students because it is rooted in fear. This mode, called *objectivism,* portrays truth as something we can achieve only by disconnecting ourselves, physically and emotionally, from the thing we want to know.

Why? Because if we get too close to it, the impure contents of our subjective lives will contaminate that thing and our knowledge of it. No matter what "it" is—an episode in history, a creature from the wild, a passage in great literature, or a phenomenon of human behavior—objectivism claims that we can know the things of the world truly and well only from afar.

For objectivism, the subjective self is the enemy most to be feared—a Pandora's box of opinion, bias, and ignorance that will distort our knowledge once the lid flies open. We keep the lid shut by relying exclusively on reason and facts, logic and data that cannot be swayed by subjective desire (or so the theory goes). The role of the mind and the senses in this scheme is not to connect us to the world but to hold the world at bay, lest our knowledge of it be tainted.

In objectivism, subjectivity is feared not only because it contaminates things but because it creates relationships between those things and us—and relationships are contaminating as well. When a thing ceases to be an object and becomes a vital, interactive part of our lives—whether it is a work of art, an indigenous people, or an ecosystem—it might get a grip on us, biasing us toward it, thus threatening the purity of our knowledge once again.

So objectivism, driven by fear, keeps us from forging relationships with the things of the world. Its modus operandi is simple: when we distance ourselves from something, it becomes an object; when it becomes an object, it no longer has life; when it is lifeless, it cannot touch or transform us, so our knowledge of the thing remains pure.

For objectivism, any way of knowing that requires subjective involvement between the knower and the known is regarded as primitive, unreliable, and even dangerous. The intuitive is derided as irrational, true feeling is dismissed as sentimental, the imagination is seen as chaotic and unruly, and storytelling is labeled as personal and pointless.

That is why music, art, and dance are at the bottom of the academic pecking order and the "hard" sciences are at the top. That is why every "soft" discipline in the curriculum has practitioners doing research that is more objectivist than thou: literary scholars who count adverbs rather than explore meanings, psychologists who analyze the data of human behavior as if people had no more inner life than Styrofoam.

Years ago, Alfred North Whitehead declared that "inert ideas" were the bane of higher education, deadening the process of teaching and learning for students and teachers alike.[6] But for objectivism, the only good idea is an inert idea that like the lepidopterist's prize butterfly is no longer elusive and on the wing but has been chloroformed, pinned, boxed, and labeled. This way of knowing may render the world lifeless—but that, say its proponents, is a small price to pay for what they call objective truth.

I have not forgotten that objectivism originated, in part, to save us from the evils of reckless subjectivity. The victims of the Black Death would have benefited from the objective knowledge that their suffering was caused by fleas from infected rats, not by offenses against God. The countless women burned at the stake because someone called them witches bear mute testimony to the cruelties that subjectivity can breed.

Objectivism set out to put truth on firmer ground than the whims of princes and priests, and for that we can be grateful. But history is full of ironies, and one of them is the way objectivism has bred new versions of the same evils it tried to correct. Two examples come quickly to mind: the rise of modern dictatorships and the character of contemporary warfare.

A good case can be made that objectivism, which intended to free people from the clutches of arbitrary power, has sometimes conspired with other forces to deliver modern people into the clutches of totalitarianism. As people became convinced that objective answers to all questions were possible—and as specialists emerged who were glad to give those answers—people began to distrust their own knowledge and turn to authorities for truth. Thus the stage was set for "authorities" with a political agenda to seize power at moments of social vulnerability, proclaiming, "I alone know the truth that will save you! Fall in and follow me."

The cruelties of modern warfare are another outcome of objectivity run amok, just as the cruelties of the witch-hunt were the consequence of subjectivity gone mad. Many Americans found the Gulf War acceptable, even popular, because it was fought with a technology that allows us to do violence to others at distances that keep us safe. We killed tens of thousands of Iraqis in the Gulf War, but all we saw were shadowy images of destruction—images that were applauded in TV rooms throughout the land, so grateful are we for the capacity to kill at great remove.

Contrast this with the war in Vietnam, which we were forced to fight up close, subjectively, a war considerably less popular with the American people than the objectivist war in the Persian Gulf. In Vietnam, our soldiers came face to face with the enemy, our civilians came face to face with the deaths of fifty thousand Americans, and we sank into a national slough of guilt and grief. When President Bush declared that our victory in the Persian Gulf had finally allowed us to "kick the Vietnam syndrome," he was celebrating the triumph of objective detachment over subjective intimacy.

Why does objectivism conspire with totalitarianism and violence? From the outset, the objectivist impulse was more than a quest for truth: it was a fear-driven overkill of the subjectivity that made the premodern world dangerous. Objectivism was never content to quarantine subjectivity in order to stop its spread. It aimed at killing the germ of "self" to secure objective truth—just as dictators kill dissenters to secure the "public order," and warriors kill the enemy to secure the "peace."

"Killing the self" is not an image of my invention. It can be found at the heart of the objectivist literature itself. A century ago, when objectivism was in full flower, the philosopher Karl Pearson wrote an influential book called *The Grammar of Science* in which he made a classic case for objective knowledge, arguing that "the habit of forming a judgment upon . . . facts unbiased by personal feeling is characteristic of what may be termed the scientific frame of mind."[7]

Unfortunately, Pearson accompanied his classic case with a classic Freudian slip: "The scientific man has above all things to strive at self-elimination in his judgments."[8] Some may call it ambiguous diction, but I call it prophecy: in the century since Pearson wrote, objectivism has pursued its goal of eliminating the self with considerable success when a student must ask if he can use "I" in an autobiography.

My case against objectivism has been normative to this point: objectivism, fearful of both the knowing self and the thing known, distances self from world and deforms our relationships with our subjects, our students, and ourselves. But an even more telling case can be made against this mode of knowing: it fails to give a faithful account of how knowing actually happens, even at the heart of science itself.

No scientist knows the world merely by holding it at arm's length: if we ever managed to build the objectivist wall between the knower and the known, we could know nothing except the wall itself. Science requires an engagement with the world, a live encounter between the knower and the known. That encounter has moments of distance, but it would not be an encounter without moments of intimacy as well.

Knowing of any sort is relational, animated by a desire to come into deeper community with what we know. Why does a historian study the "dead" past? To reveal how much of it lives in us today. Why does a biologist study the "mute" world of nature? To allow us to hear its voice speaking of how entwined we are in life's ecology. Why does a literary scholar study the world of "fiction"? To show us that the facts can never be understood except in communion with the imagination.

Knowing is how we make community with the unavailable other, with realities that would elude us without the connective tissue of knowledge. Knowing is a human way to seek relationship and, in the process, to have encounters and exchanges that will inevitably alter us. At its deepest reaches, knowing is always communal.

The now-famous story of biologist Barbara McClintock illumines the fact that we know by connecting with the world, not by disconnecting from it. McClintock, who died in 1992 at age ninety, became fascinated early in her career with the mysteries of genetic transposition. Though her research was often dismissed as wildly unorthodox, she pursued it into discoveries that changed the map of modern genetics, and she was honored in 1983 with a Nobel Prize.

McClintock did not objectify her subject, did not approach it with the textbook notion that her task was to analyze it into data bits. Instead, she approached genetic material on the assumption that it could best be understood as a communal phenomenon. As one writer has said, McClintock "made a crucial discovery by recognizing that the genetics of living organisms is more complex and interdependent than anyone had believed. By observing how genes function in their environment rather than regarding them merely as isolated entities, she discovered that bits of genes can move about on chromosomes."[9]

When Evelyn Fox Keller interviewed McClintock in order to write her biography, it became clear that the communal premise of McClintock's work went well beyond the relationship among genes: it included the relationship between the genes and the scientist who studied them.

Keller wanted to know, "What enabled McClintock to see further and deeper into the mysteries of genetics than her colleagues?" McClintock's answer, Keller tells us, is simple: "Over and over again she tells us one must have the time to look, the patience to 'hear what the material has to say to you,' the openness to 'let it come to you.' Above all, one must have 'a feeling for the organism.'"[10]

Of course, McClintock's science was distinguished by precise analytical thinking and impeccable data; one does not win a Nobel Prize without them. But data and logic and the distance they provide are only one pole of the paradox of great science. When McClintock, arguably the greatest biologist of our century, is asked to name the heart of her knowing, she invariably uses the language of relationship, of connectedness, of community. As one commentator puts it, McClintock "gained valuable knowledge by empathizing with her corn plants, submerging herself in their world and dissolving the boundary between object and observer."[11]

Keller sums up McClintock's genius, and the genius of all great knowing, in a single, luminous sentence: McClintock, in her relation to ears of corn, achieved "the highest form of love, love that allows for intimacy without the annihilation of difference."[12]

These remarkable words describe not only the heart of Barbara McClintock's science but also the heart of every authentic relationship that a human being might have—with history, with nature, with other people, with things of the spirit. They describe a way of knowing and of living that has moved beyond fear of the other into respect for, even a need for, its otherness.

The real agenda driving objectivism is not to tell the truth about knowing but to shore up our self-aggrandizing myth that knowledge is power and that with it we can run the world. People often lie in an effort to deny their fears—and objectivism lies about both our knowledge and our power in hopes of avoiding the distressing evidence before our own eyes: we are ruining, not running, the world.

Modern knowledge has allowed us to manipulate the world but not to control its fate (to say nothing of our own), a fact that becomes more clear each day as the ecosystem dies and our human systems fail. Indeed, by disconnecting us from the world, objectivism has led us into actions so inharmonious with reality that catastrophe seems inevitable if we stay the course. Objectivism, far from telling the truth about how we know, is a myth meant to feed our fading fantasy of science, technology, power, and control.

If we dare to move through our fear, to practice knowing as a form of love, we might abandon our illusion of control and enter a partnership with the otherness of the world. By finding our place in the ecosystem of reality, we might see more clearly which actions are life-giving and which are not—and in the process participate more fully in our own destinies, and the destiny of the world, than we do in our drive for control. This relational way of knowing—in which love takes away fear and co-creation replaces control—is a way of knowing that can help us reclaim the capacity for connectedness on which good teaching depends.

BE NOT AFRAID

Fear is everywhere—in our culture, in our institutions, in our students, in ourselves—and it cuts us off from everything. Surrounded and invaded by fear, how can we transcend it and reconnect with reality for the sake of teaching and learning? The only path I know that might take us in that direction is the one marked "spiritual."

Fear is so fundamental to the human condition that all the great spiritual traditions originate in an effort to overcome its effects on our lives. With different words, they all proclaim the same core message: "Be not afraid." Though the traditions vary widely in the ways they propose to take us beyond fear, all hold out the same hope: we can escape fear's paralysis and enter a state of grace where encounters with otherness will not threaten us but will enrich our work and our lives.

It is important to note with care what that core teaching does and does not say. "Be not afraid" does not say that we should not *have* fears—and if it did, we could dismiss it as an impossible counsel of perfection. Instead, it says that we do not need to *be* our fears, quite a different proposition.

As a young teacher, I yearned for the day when I would know my craft so well, be so competent, so experienced, and so powerful, that I could walk into any classroom without feeling afraid. But now, in my late fifties, I know that day will never come. I will always have fears, but I need not be my fears—for there are other places in my inner landscape from which I can speak and act.

Each time I walk into a classroom, I can choose the place within myself from which my teaching will come, just as I can choose the place within my students toward which my teaching will be aimed. I need not teach from a fearful place: I can teach from curiosity or hope or empathy or honesty, places that are as real within me as are my fears. I can have fear, but I need not be fear—if I am willing to stand someplace else in my inner landscape.

We yearn for a different place to stand, and I know of no better description of that yearning than the Rilke poem quoted at the head of the Introduction:

> Ah, not to be cut off,
> not through the slightest partition
> shut out from the law of the stars.
> The inner—what is it?
> if not intensified sky,
> hurled through with birds and deep
> with the winds of homecoming.[13]

"Cut off" is our customary state of being. But there is within us the constant yearning for connectedness, a yearning—"Ah!"—to live without the slightest partition between our souls and the distant stars, between ourselves and the world's otherness. We yearn for community with the other because we know that with it we would feel more at home in our lives, no longer strangers to one another and aliens to the earth.

But the "homecoming" of which Rilke speaks has two qualities that make it quite different from our conventional image of home. First, it is inner, not outer. This home is not a place that we can own—but by the same token, we cannot be banned from it, and it cannot be stolen from us. No matter where we are or what condition we are in or how many obstacles are before us, we can always come back home through a simple inward turning.

Second, when we make that inward turn, the home we find is not a closed and parochial place in which we can hide, from which we can neither see nor be seen. Instead, this home is as open and vast as the sky itself. Here we are at home with more than our own familiar thoughts and those people who think like us. We are at home in a universe that embraces both the smallness of "I" and the vastness of all that is "not I," and does so with consummate ease. In this home, we know ourselves not as isolated atoms threatened by otherness but as integral parts of the great web of life. In that knowing, we are taken beyond fear toward wholeness.

In response to the question "How can we move beyond the fear that destroys connectedness?" I am saying, "By reclaiming the connectedness that takes away fear." I realize the circularity of my case—but that is precisely how the spiritual life moves, in circles that have no beginning or end, where, as Eliot writes, we "arrive where we started/And know the place for the first time."[14] The only question is whether we choose to stand outside of the circle or within it.

How do we get into that circle? When we are gripped by the fears that keep us disconnected, what will move us toward joining hands with others? The truth is that the circle is already in us.

In the human psyche, apparent opposites chase each other around in circles all the time: love and hate, laughter and tears, fear and desire. Our intense fear of connectedness, and the challenges it brings, is pursued by an equally intense desire for connectedness, and the comforts it offers. For all the fearful efforts we make to protect ourselves by disconnecting, the human soul yearns eternally for connection: "Ah, not to be cut off . . ." We can get into the circle that is already within us by abandoning ourselves to the yearnings that run just behind, or ahead of, our fears.

Sometimes all it takes is a simple step. In a group of experienced K–12 teachers I worked with for two years was a high school shop teacher, six feet six inches tall, weighing 240 pounds, athletic and deep of voice. No one ever thought of this man as afraid, not even the man himself.

For several years, the principal at his school had been pressing the teacher to attend a summer institute on technology. The shop curriculum, said the principal, had to be modernized, and quickly, or the students would be lost in the past.

Nonsense, this fearless teacher replied. The technology touted at that institute is probably just a fad. Even if it isn't, high school students need to learn the basics—hands-on work with materials and tools. There will be plenty of time later on for fancy refinements of their technique.

The shop teacher and his principal became locked in a demoralizing cycle of demands and refusals, each exacerbating the other. Their relations grew adversarial and strained. As the shop teacher participated in our group, that brokenness weighed heavy on his heart.

Then one day the shop teacher came to a meeting and told us that the cycle had been broken. His principal had called him in to make his demands once more. This time, instead of arguing the merits of the traditional shop curriculum, the teacher looked at his principal and said, "I still don't want to go to that institute, but now I know why. I'm afraid—afraid I won't understand it, afraid my field has passed me by, afraid I am a has-been as a teacher."

There was a silence, and then the principal spoke: "I'm afraid, too," he said. "Let's go to the institute together."

They did, and they reclaimed and deepened their friendship, and the shop teacher feels he is making progress toward modernizing the curriculum and revitalizing his vocation.

This teacher's breakthrough did not directly involve adopting a new technique for teaching; indeed, it did not directly involve *doing* anything at all. His breakthrough was into a new way of *being,* into the realization that he could have fear but did not need to be fear— that he could speak and act from a place of honesty about being fearful rather than from the fear itself.

The shop teacher honored a yearning within himself that was just behind, or ahead of, his fear, the yearning not to be cut off from his principal, his students, his world of work, or his teacher's heart. Sometimes the way beyond fear is just that simple.

Chapter III

The Hidden Wholeness

Paradox in Teaching and Learning

There is in all visible things
an invisible fecundity,
a dimmed light,
a meek namelessness,
a hidden wholeness.
This mysterious Unity and Integrity
is Wisdom, the Mother of all,
Natura naturans.

—THOMAS MERTON, "HAGIA SOPHIA"[1]

THINKING THE WORLD TOGETHER

The culture of disconnection that undermines teaching and learning is driven partly by fear. But it is also driven by our Western commitment to thinking in polarities, a thought form that elevates disconnection into an intellectual virtue. This way of thinking is so embedded in our culture that we rarely escape it, even when we try—and my own words will prove the point.

In earlier chapters, I tried to correct several imbalances in the way we approach teaching. To correct our overemphasis on technique, I stressed the teacher's identity and integrity. To correct our obsession with objective knowledge, I stressed subjective engagement. To correct our excessive regard for the powers of intellect, I stressed the power of emotions to freeze, or free, the mind.

My intent was to rebalance the scales. But in a polarizing culture, it is hard to do that without slamming the scales in the opposite direction. In arguing for the neglected pole, I may be mistaken for someone who excuses poor technique, urging teachers just to "be themselves"; who believes there are no standards for truth, just "whatever you think it is"; who doesn't care about the content of your thoughts, just as long as you "share what you feel."

It is obvious (I hope!) that these are distortions of what I have said. But we distort things this way all the time because we are trained neither to voice both sides of an issue nor to listen with both ears. The problem goes deeper than the bad habit of competitive conversation some of us have: tell me your thesis and I will find any way, fair or foul, to argue the other side! It is rooted in the fact that we look at the world through analytical lenses. We see everything as this or that, plus or minus, on or off, black or white; and we fragment reality into an endless series of *either-ors*. In a phrase, we think the world apart.

Thinking the world apart, like thinking at a distance, has given us great power. Just as I respect the power of objectivity, rightly understood, I respect the power of analysis—in its rightful place. I have used analytical tools to develop my thesis in this book, and the remarkable machine on which I am writing it is driven by millions upon millions of either-or decisions. Without binary logic, we would have neither computers nor many of the gifts of modern science.

But for all the power it has given us in science and technology, either-or thinking has also given us a fragmented sense of reality that destroys the wholeness and wonder of life. Our problem is compounded by the fact that this mode of knowing has become normative in nearly every area, even though it misleads and betrays us when applied to the perennial problems of being human that lie beyond the reach of logic.

How can we escape the grip of either-or thinking? What would it look like to "think the world together," not to abandon discriminatory logic where it serves us well but to develop a more capacious habit of mind that supports the capacity for connectedness on which good teaching depends?

Niels Bohr, the Nobel Prize–winning physicist, offers the keystone I want to build on: "The opposite of a true statement is a false statement, but the opposite of a profound truth can be another profound truth."[2]

With a few well-chosen words, Bohr defines a concept that is essential to thinking the world together—the concept of paradox. In certain circumstances, truth is found not by splitting the world into either-ors but by embracing it as *both-and*. In certain circumstances, truth is a paradoxical joining of apparent opposites, and if we want to know that truth, we must learn to embrace those opposites as one.

In the empirical world, as Bohr makes clear, there are choices to be made between true and false, choices that must be informed by fact and reason. If the question before us is whether a particular tree is an oak or a maple, we can examine its pedigree in full confidence that it cannot be both and that certain empirical markers will reveal what kind it is.

But Bohr also affirms another realm of knowing where binary logic misleads us. This is the realm of "profound truth," where, if we want to know what is essential, we must stop thinking the world into pieces and start thinking it together again.

Profound truth, rather than empirical fact, is the stuff of which paradoxes are made. But profound need not mean exotic or esoteric. We encounter paradoxical profundities every day simply because we are human, for we ourselves are paradoxes that breathe! Indeed, breathing itself is a form of paradox, requiring inhaling and exhaling to be whole.

The first two chapters of this book are full of ordinary truths about teaching that can be expressed only as paradoxes:

- The knowledge I have gained from thirty years of teaching goes hand in hand with my sense of being a rank amateur at the start of each new class.

- My inward and invisible sense of identity becomes known, even to me, only as it manifests itself in encounters with external and visible "otherness."

- Good teaching comes from identity, not technique, but if I allow my identity to guide me toward an integral technique, that technique can help me express my identity more fully.

- Teaching always takes place at the crossroads of the personal and the public, and if I want to teach well, I must learn to stand where these opposites intersect.

- Intellect works in concert with feeling, so if I hope to open my students' minds, I must open their emotions as well.

None of these truths about teaching can be approached as a simple either-or, though in academic culture we constantly try to do so. When I speak with faculty about the fear students bring into the classroom and how it paralyzes their ability to learn, often some critic will say, "So, you want us to stop being professors and become therapists."

No, that is not what I want. What I want is a richer, more paradoxical model of teaching and learning than binary thought allows, a model that reveals how the paradox of thinking and feeling are joined—whether we are comfortable with paradox or not.

Behind the critic's comment is a trained incapacity to see that heart and mind work as one in our students and in ourselves. They cannot be treated separately, one by the professor, the other by the therapist. When a person is healthy and whole, the head and the heart are both-and, not either-or, and teaching that honors that paradox can help make us all more whole.

When Things Fall Apart

It takes training to think the world apart because we arrive in this world with an instinctive capacity to hold paradoxes together. Watch a young child go through the day, and you will see how action and rest, thought and feeling, tears and laughter are intimate and inseparable companions.

In a child, the opposites commingle and co-create each other with the animal fluidity of breathing in and out. But that easy embrace of paradox is soon drummed out of us. Early in our journey toward adulthood, we are taught that survival depends on our ability to dissect life and discriminate among its parts.

The ability to discriminate is important—but only where the failure to do so will get us into trouble. A child must learn the difference between hot and cold to keep from getting hurt and the difference between right and wrong to keep from hurting others. But it is equally important that we retain, or recover, the ability to embrace paradox where discrimination will get us into trouble—the kind of trouble we get into when we enter adulthood with partitions between thinking and feeling, personal and professional, shadow and light.

THE COURAGE TO TEACH

We split paradoxes so reflexively that we do not understand the price we pay for our habit. The poles of a paradox are like the poles of a battery: hold them together, and they generate the energy of life; pull them apart, and the current stops flowing. When we separate any of the profound paired truths of our lives, both poles become lifeless specters of themselves—and we become lifeless as well. Dissecting a living paradox has the same impact on our intellectual, emotional, and spiritual well-being as the decision to breathe in without ever breathing out would have on our physical health.

Consider our paradoxical need for both community and solitude. Human beings were made for relationships: without a rich and nourishing network of connections, we wither and die. I am not speaking metaphorically. It is a clinical fact that people who lack relationships get sick more often and recover more slowly than people surrounded by family and friends.

At the same time, we were made for solitude. Our lives may be rich in relationships, but the human self remains a mystery of enfolded inwardness that no other person can possibly enter or know. If we fail to embrace our ultimate aloneness and seek meaning only in communion with others, we wither and die. Other-directedness may serve us well in certain roles or at certain stages of life, but the farther we travel toward the great mystery, the more at home we must be with our essential aloneness in order to stay healthy and whole.

Our equal and opposite needs for solitude and community constitute a great paradox. When it is torn apart, both of these life-giving states of being degenerate into deathly specters of themselves. Solitude split off from community is no longer a rich and fulfilling experience of inwardness; now it becomes loneliness, a terrible isolation. Community split off from solitude is no longer a nurturing network of relationships; now it becomes a crowd, an alienating buzz of too many people and too much noise.

As Dietrich Bonhoeffer said, "Let [the person] who cannot be alone beware of community. Let [the person] who is not in community beware of being alone."[3] In a culture that rips paradoxes apart, many people know nothing of the rich dialectic of solitude and community; they know only a daily whiplash between loneliness and the crowd.

We even have personality technologies to make the whiplash stronger. I am thinking of the psychological tests we use, or misuse, to categorize ourselves as personality "types." Am I introverted or extroverted, inner-directed or other-directed, intuitive or sensate, feminine (and made for community) or masculine (and made for competition)? We put ourselves in either-or boxes, or are put there by others, and fail to embrace the paradoxical nature of the human self.

The world of education as we know it is filled with broken paradoxes—and with the lifeless results:

- We separate head from heart. Result: minds that do not know how to feel and hearts that do not know how to think.
- We separate facts from feelings. Result: bloodless facts that make the world distant and remote and ignorant emotions that reduce truth to how one feels today.
- We separate theory from practice. Result: theories that have little to do with life and practice that is uninformed by understanding.
- We separate teaching from learning. Result: teachers who talk but do not listen and students who listen but do not talk.

Paradoxical thinking requires that we embrace a view of the world in which opposites are joined, so that we can see the world clearly and see it whole. Such a view is characterized by neither flinty-eyed realism nor dewy-eyed romanticism but rather by a creative synthesis of the two.

The result is a world more complex and confusing than the one made simple by either-or thought—but that simplicity is merely the dullness of death. When we think things together, we reclaim the life force in the world, in our students, in ourselves.

THE LIMITS AND POTENTIALS OF SELF

Paradox is not only an abstract mode of knowing. It is a lens through which we can learn more about the selfhood from which good teaching comes.

In workshops on teaching and learning, I invite faculty to look at their own classroom practice through the lens of paradox. I ask each teacher to write brief descriptions of two recent moments in teaching: a moment when things were going so well that you knew you were born to teach and a moment when things were going so poorly that you wished you had never been born.

Remembering such moments is the first step in exploring one of the true paradoxes of teaching: the same person who teaches brilliantly one day can be an utter flop the next! Though we normally take that paradox in a fatalistic or self-mocking manner, in this exercise we are asked to take it seriously as a source of self-knowledge.

Next, I ask people to gather in groups of three to focus on the positive case and help each group member in turn identify his or her gifts—that is, to name the strengths and capacities of the teacher that helped make the case in question an authentic learning experience.

Conducting this exercise on paper, as I am about to attempt, is not nearly as engaging as doing it face to face. I hope you will try it with a few colleagues, if for no other reason than the opportunity it offers to affirm one another as teachers, something we rarely do. Not only does the exercise help us understand ourselves in the light of paradox, but it can deepen our sense of collegiality as well.

Here is a moment from my own teaching experience at a small college in Appalachia, whose students come primarily from that economically depressed region:

In my 1 P.M. senior seminar, we had been reading *Habits of the Heart* by Robert Bellah and his colleagues,[4] whose main themes I had outlined in a lecture the preceding session. Now I wanted us to take the book's thesis that expressive individualism has replaced community and tradition—a thesis built largely on data from the urban North— and test it against the experience of these students from Appalachia.

I asked them—first in small groups, guided by focus questions, and then in our large group, guided by me—to explore what they had been taught and what they believed about "freedom" (one of the key elements of individualism explored in *Habits*), especially "freedom from . . ." and "freedom to . . ." The small groups seemed very animated, and in the large group, more than three-fourths of the students contributed to an open and engaging discussion.

Most of them said the same thing: they wanted "freedom from" things like unhealthy family ties, narrow religious beliefs, and prejudiced communities, and they wanted "freedom to" be themselves, choose for themselves, express themselves, and even "be selfish." Their comments seemed to fit the *Habits* thesis perfectly—and yet I had the sense that there was more to their lives than they were able, or willing, to articulate.

Then one of the students—a popular young man, well known on campus for his religious faith and humane spirit—found some excuse (I cannot remember what it was) to tell the story of his false arrest earlier that term for drug-dealing in what turned out to be a case of mistaken identity. Given his character and the irony of his arrest, it was a very funny story, and he had everyone laughing uproariously until I intervened with a question: "Why didn't you sue the police for false arrest? You might have gotten rich overnight."

The room quieted while the student explained that he would never have sued, that he was just happy that his mistaken identity had eventually been cleared up. Then, defending and excusing the police, he said, "Everyone makes mistakes." Almost all the other students quickly made it clear that they agreed with his moral position.

I pursued the inquiry: "Let me hold a mirror up to you. You talk in terms of individualism and self-seeking, but underneath all of that you have such a strong sense of communal membership that you are willing to forgive the police their mistake rather than try to make money off of it. The kind of individualism the authors of *Habits* are talking about is not softened by that sense of community. The stereotypical individualist would have hired a lawyer that evening and filed suit the next morning."

In discussion, the class members seemed to find this interesting and insightful, and they agreed that this mix of individualism and community described them well. I ended up feeling that together we had accomplished two things: a deeper understanding of the book and a deeper understanding of the students' lives. I also had a sense of what the next item on our agenda should be: Why the gap between their individualistic rhetoric and their instinctively communal behavior?

What gifts do I possess that helped make this moment possible? Answering that question here may seem a bit self-congratulatory. I ask only that you reserve judgment until you read my second case. Then it will become clear that there is less to me than my gifts!

Here are some of the strengths other teachers have ascribed to me when I have offered this case in workshops:

- A capacity to combine structure or intentionality with flexibility in both planning and leading the class: clarity about my objectives but openness to various ways of achieving them
- Thorough knowledge of the material I assigned to my students and a commitment to helping them master that material too
- A desire to help my students build a bridge between the academic text and their own lives and a strategic approach for doing so
- A respect for my students' stories that is no more or less than my respect for the scholarly texts I assigned to them
- An ability to see my students' lives more clearly than they themselves see them, a capacity to look beyond their initial self-presentation, and a desire to help them see themselves more deeply
- An aptitude for asking good questions and listening carefully to my student's responses—not only to what they say but also to what they leave unsaid
- A willingness to take risks, especially the risk of inviting open dialogue, though I can never know where it is going to take us

Receiving such affirmation is like getting a massage, which is reason enough to welcome it. But there are two additional and important reasons for doing so. First, becoming aware of our gifts can help us teach more consistently from our identity and integrity. Acknowledging our gifts is difficult for many of us, either because we are modest or because it is risky to stick one's head up. But when we are not reminded of and honored for the gifts we bring to teaching, it is easy for us to revert to the dominant pedagogy, even if it has little relation to who we are.

Second, we need reassurance about our gifts in order to take the next step—examining, with others, a moment when our teaching became all pain and no joy. Looking at our "failings" is always hard, but it is easier when done against the backdrop of our strengths. It can even be fruitful, as I hope to show in a moment, when we use paradox to transform a litany of failings into a deeper understanding of the identity from which good teaching comes.

Here is my second case. It comes from the same college, the same semester, and the same course, though a different section—thus proving that you never step into the same stream twice!

In my 3 P.M. senior seminar class, I was troubled from day one by a sense that a fair number of my students were cynical about what we were doing and were determined to stay disengaged. No matter what I tried, their entire emotional range seemed to go from silly to sullen to silent.

Three young women in particular behaved in junior high school mode, passing notes back and forth, ignoring printed items I circulated for discussion, talking to each other during both lectures and discussions, rolling their eyes in response to comments made by me and by other students, and so on. The whole class annoyed me, but these three were a particular needle in my eye.

After several sessions, I spoke to the class, said I was not happy with how it was going, named the behaviors I found distracting, and asked people to tell me what I needed to change—or else to get engaged with what we were doing. No one made any suggestions for changes, and as time went on, some students became marginally more involved with the class. But the Gang of Three continued to misbehave.

So I confronted them outside of class one afternoon when I happened to run into them on campus. "Confronted" is not an excessive characterization—I spoke with anger. They responded by telling me three things:(1) I should not "take it all so personally"; (2) I had made a mistake by disagreeing too vigorously with something one of them had said in class, which had made her mad at me; and (3) they were seniors who were tired of the college's required courses, of which mine was one, and had decided before the term even began to "blow it off."

All of that added to my anger, so I kept pressing for an apology until I got one. At that point, I apologized for my anger (which I realized was excessive, because I had become obsessed with these three) and suggested that perhaps we could start over. The young women agreed to try—probably to keep me from blowing up again.

Following that encounter, one of the three made a few real contributions to the class, but the other two—though they stopped misbehaving—remained disengaged. The class as a whole was dull and distracted, and I simply wanted to get the whole thing over with. I had found my sea legs with the group and was no longer thrown off by anyone, simply because I had lowered my expectations for any given session: *I made peace with the class by giving up on it.* I hate to teach, or live, that way, but with this group, that seemed to be the only way out.

I have reread and relived this miserable episode many times. It causes me so much pain and embarrassment that I always try to leap quickly from the debacle to the natural question, "What could I have done differently that might have made for a better outcome?" But when I lead this exercise in workshops, I insist that participants avoid that question like the plague.

The question is natural only because we are naturally evasive: by asking the question too soon, we try to jump out of our pain into the "fixes" of technique. To take a hard experience like this and leap immediately to "practical solutions" is to evade the insight into one's identity that is always available in moments of vulnerability—insight that comes only as we are willing to dwell more deeply in the dynamics that made us vulnerable.

Eventually, the how-to question is worth asking. But understanding my identity is the first and crucial step in finding new ways to teach: nothing I do differently as a teacher will make any difference to anyone if it is not rooted in my nature.

So I ask the small groups to look at this second case in the light of a particular paradox: every gift a person possesses goes hand in hand with a liability. Every strength is also a weakness, a limitation, a dimension of identity that serves me and others well under some circumstances but not all the time. If my gift is a powerful analytical mind, I have an obvious asset with problems that yield to rationality. But if the problem at hand is an emotional tangle with another person and I use my gift to try to analyze the problem away, the liabilities that accompany my gift will quickly become clear.

What are we to do with the limits we find on the flip side of our gifts? The point is not to "get fixed" but to gain deeper understanding of the paradox of gifts and limits, the paradox of our mixed selves, so that we can teach, and live, more gracefully within the whole of our nature.

When I explore my second case with fellow teachers, I always learn important things about my teaching, as long as my colleagues are able to avoid the fix-it mode. Most important, I learn that my gift as a teacher is the ability to dance with my students, to co-create with them a context in which all of us can teach and learn, and that this gift works as long as I stay open and trusting and hopeful about who my students are.

But when my students refuse to dance with me, my strength turns to weakness. I get angry, although my relational nature often keeps me from expressing my anger in clean and open ways. I become silently resentful and start stepping on the toes of my unwilling dance partners, occasionally kicking their shins. I become closed and untrusting and hopeless far more quickly than need be, simply because they have rejected my gift.

I have no wish to learn distanced methods of teaching simply to satisfy students who do not want to relate to me: teaching from afar would violate my own identity and integrity and only worsen the situation. Instead, I want to learn how to hold the paradoxical poles of my identity together, to embrace the profoundly opposite truths that my sense of self is deeply dependent on others dancing with me *and* that I still have a self when no one wants to dance.

Using *and* rather than *but* in that sentence is important because it expresses a true paradox. My sense of self is so deeply dependent on others that I will always suffer a bit when others refuse to relate to me; there is no way around that simple fact. At the same time, I still have a self when relationships fail—and the suffering I experience is evidence of it.

I need to learn that the pain I sometimes experience in teaching is as much a sign that my selfhood is alive and well as the joy I feel when the dance is in full swing. If I learn that simple but profound truth, I might stay closer to my gift and farther from repressed anger and be more likely to teach in ways that will work for both me and my students.

The root cause of this low point in my teaching was not a failure of technique, though there are techniques that could help me in such moments. The root cause was a sense of self-negation, or even self-annihilation, that came when my students were unwilling to help me fulfill my nature.

It is embarrassing to put it that baldly. I know, intellectually, how naive it is to assume that other people, especially students, are here to help me fulfill myself—naive at best and arrogant at worst. But that assumption is what did me in as that class unraveled, and my own growth as a teacher requires that I face such awkward facts.

To become a better teacher, I must nurture a sense of self that both does *and* does not depend on the responses of others—and that is a true paradox. To learn that lesson well, I must take a solitary journey into my own nature *and* seek the help of others in seeing myself as I am—another of the many paradoxes that abound on the inner terrain.

PARADOX AND PEDAGOGICAL DESIGN

The principle of paradox is not a guide only to the complexities and potentials of selfhood. It can also guide us in thinking about classroom dynamics and in designing the kind of teaching and learning space that can hold a classroom session.

By *space* I mean a complex of factors: the physical arrangement and feeling of the room, the conceptual framework that I build around the topic my students and I are exploring, the emotional ethos I hope to facilitate, and the ground rules that will guide our inquiry. The space that works best for me is one shaped by a series of paradoxes, and I think I understand why.

Teaching and learning require a higher degree of awareness than we ordinarily possess—and awareness is always heightened when we are caught in a creative tension. Paradox is another name for that tension, a way of holding opposites together that creates an electric charge that keeps us awake. Not all good teachers use the same technique, but whatever technique they use, good teachers always find ways to induce this creative tension.

When I design a classroom session, I am aware of six paradoxical tensions that I want to build into the teaching and learning space. These six are neither prescriptive nor exhaustive. They are simply mine, offered to illustrate how the principle of paradox might contribute to pedagogical design:

1. The space should be bounded and open.
2. The space should be hospitable and "charged."
3. The space should invite the voice of the individual and the voice of the group.
4. The space should honor the "little" stories of the students and the "big" stories of the disciplines and tradition.
5. The space should support solitude and surround it with the resources of community.
6. The space should welcome both silence and speech.

I want to say a few words about what each of these paradoxes means. Then, to rescue the paradoxes and the reader from death by abstraction, I want to explore some practical ways for classroom teachers to bring these idea to life.

1. *The space should be bounded and open.* The boundaries around a teaching and learning space are created by using a question, a text, or a body of data that keeps us focused on the subject at hand. Within those boundaries, students are free to speak, but their speaking is always guided toward the topic, not only by the teacher but also by the materials at hand. Those materials must be so clear and compelling that students will find it hard to wander from the subject— even when it confuses or frightens them and they would prefer to evade its demands. Space without boundaries is not space, it is a chaotic void, and in such a place no learning is likely to occur.

But for a space to be a space, it must be open as well as bounded—open to the many paths down which discovery may take us, to the surprises that always come with real learning. If boundaries remind us that our journey has a destination, openness reminds us that there are many ways to reach that end. Deeper still, the openness of a learning space reminds us that the destination we plotted at the outset of the journey may not be the one we will reach, that we must stay alert for clues to our true destination as we travel together.

2. *The space should be hospitable and "charged."* Open space is liberating, but it also raises the fear of getting lost in the uncharted and the unknown. So a learning space must be hospitable—inviting as well as open, safe and trustworthy as well as free. The boundaries around the space offer some of that reassurance, but when those boundaries hold us to difficult topics, additional reassurance is required. So a learning space must have features that help students deal with the dangers of an educational expedition: places to rest, places to find nourishment, even places to seek shelter when one feels overexposed.

But if that expedition is to take us somewhere, the space must also be charged. If students are to learn at the deepest levels, they must not feel so safe that they fall asleep: they need to feel the risks inherent in pursuing the deep things of the world or of the soul. No special effects are required to create this charge—it comes with the territory. We only need fence the space, fill it with topics of significance, and refuse to let anyone evade or trivialize them.

3. *The space should invite the voice of the individual and the voice of the group.* If a space is to support learning, it must invite students to find their authentic voices, whether or not they speak in ways approved by others. Learning does not happen when students are unable to express their ideas, emotions, confusions, ignorance, and prejudices. In fact, only when people can speak their minds does education have a chance to happen.

But a teaching and learning space must be more than a forum for individual expression. It must also be a place in which the group's voice is gathered and amplified, so that the group can affirm, question, challenge, and correct the voice of the individual. The teacher's

The Hidden Wholeness

task is to listen for what the group voice is saying and to play that voice back from time to time so the group can hear and even change its own collective mind.

The paradox of individual and collective voices is most clearly illustrated by an example from outside the classroom: making decisions by consensus. Here, no decision can be made as long as even one voice dissents, so the group must learn to listen to individuals with care. But as a corporate voice emerges through honest dialogue, the group makes a claim on each person, compelling us neither to roll over nor to be defiant but to seek, and speak, our truth more thoughtfully. In a learning space shaped by this paradox, not only do students learn about a subject, but they also learn to speak their own thoughts about that subject and to listen for an emergent collective wisdom that may influence their ideas and beliefs.

4.   *The space should honor the "little" stories of the individual and the "big" stories of the disciplines and tradition.* A learning space should not be filled with abstractions so bloated that no room remains for the small but soulful realities that grow in our students' lives. In this space there must be ample room for the little stories of individuals, stories of personal experience in which the student's inner teacher is at work.

But when my little story, or yours, is our only point of reference, we easily become lost in narcissism. So the big stories of the disciplines must also be told in the learning space—stories that are universal in scope and archetypal in depth, that frame our personal tales and help us understand what they mean. We must help students learn to listen to the big stories with the same respect we accord individuals when they tell us the tales of their lives.

5.   *The space should support solitude and surround it with the resources of community.* Learning demands solitude—not only in the sense that students need time alone to reflect and absorb but also in the deeper sense that the integrity of the student's inner self must be respected, not violated, if we expect the student to learn. Learning also demands community—a dialogical exchange in which our ignorance can be aired, our ideas tested, our biases challenged, and our knowledge expanded, an exchange in which we are not simply left alone to think our own thoughts.

But there are forms, or perversions, of community that are inimical to deep solitude, that do not respect interiority and are invasive of the soul. When the group norm asserts, however subtly, that everyone must speak, or must speak in a common voice, then both speech and dissent are stifled, the solitude of the individual is violated, and no learning can occur.

An authentic learning community is not just compatible with solitude; it is essential to a full realization of what the inner teacher is trying to tell us. In a community that respects the mystery of the soul, we help each other remove impediments to discernment. Given certain sensibilities and safeguards, nourished and protected by a teacher, a learning community can help us see both barriers and openings to the truth that lives within us.

6. *The space should welcome both silence and speech.* Words are not the sole medium of exchange in teaching and learning—we educate with silence as well. Silence gives us a chance to reflect on what we have said and heard, and silence itself can be a sort of speech, emerging from the deepest parts of ourselves, of others, of the world.

Psychologists say that a typical group can abide about fifteen seconds of silence before someone feels the need to break the tension by speaking. It is our old friend fear at work, interpreting the silence as something gone wrong, certain that worthwhile things will not happen if we are not making noise. But in authentic education, silence is treated as a trustworthy matrix for the inner work students must do, a medium for learning of the deepest sort.

These six paradoxes add up to sound pedagogy—in theory. But what do they look like in practice? I will try to answer that question, with one proviso: what follows is not a "formula" for teaching but rather a personal account of how I have tried to hold these paradoxes together in my own work.

The principle of paradox can help illumine the selfhood of any teacher and the construction of any teaching and learning space, but the particular pedagogy I am about to describe emerges from a selfhood that may bear scant resemblance to your own. By saying yes— or no, or maybe—to what follows, you may discover something about the sources of teaching that have authenticity for you.

PRACTICING PARADOX IN THE CLASSROOM

To show how these six paradoxes might be implemented in the classroom, I want to look in detail at the moment described in my first case study—in full awareness of the humility required by my second case! When I sat down to plan the session described in case one, I began with the first paradox: the learning space should be open and bounded. To implement that principle, I turned to the text we were reading at that point in the course, *Habits of the Heart.*

A good text embodies both openness and boundaries—the boundaries created by a clear and compelling set of issues and the openness that comes from exploring those issues in a reflective manner. By choosing such a text and immersing myself in it, I can often get a sense of the learning space I want to create in class. So I reviewed the issues central to *Habits,* finally settling on what Americans believe about freedom as the one I wanted to pursue.

But taking pedagogical clues from a text does not imply slavish adherence to it; the most boring classes I ever took (or taught) stayed so close to the text that we might as well have stayed home. By a good text I mean one that is fundamentally sound and—another paradox—one with enough unexplained gaps that it cannot be followed like a cookbook.

Students do not learn to learn from a text that is without sin, one that raises all the right questions and gives all the right answers. But a text with discontinuities and ambiguities demands our engagement, giving students space to move into its field of discourse and think their own thoughts. Taking pedagogical clues from a text means looking not only for what the text can teach us but also for what we can teach the text.

Habits of the Heart, it seems to me, is blessed by certain gaps in its data, which are based on interviews with a narrow range of Americans from which the authors draw some wide-ranging conclusions. From my vantage point at a small Appalachian college, I was aware that *Habits* had little to say about the large number of Americans who live in poverty and nothing at all to say about the unique experience of poverty in Appalachia.

To honor the first paradox—a learning space should be open and bounded—I decided to create boundaries by asking my students to focus on the picture of freedom that *Habits* paints and then to open that space by asking them, "What's wrong with this picture?" based on their own experience. (Of course, the questioning approach itself honors the first paradox by creating clear boundaries around the subject while leaving students free to make their own responses.)

By inviting data from my students' lives into the conversation, I was honoring that part of the second paradox that says the learning space should be hospitable. Hospitality in the classroom requires not only that we treat our students with civility and compassion but also that we invite our students and their insights into the conversation. The good host is not merely polite to the guest—the good host assumes that the guest has stories to tell.

This second paradox requires that a learning space be charged as well as hospitable, a space where students are challenged as well as welcomed. I hoped to create this charge by lifting up freedom as the concept I wanted my students to reflect on. I knew that freedom was a major issue in their lives: some were still rebelling against their families, and others felt that the college unduly constrained their lives.

So my focus questions—"What have you been taught in the past about freedom, especially 'freedom from' and 'freedom to'? And what beliefs about freedom do you now hold?"—were chosen because I thought they might be hot buttons, and so they were. They got my students' attention, emotionally and intellectually, drawing them so deeply into the learning space that they could hardly avoid the challenge to think real thoughts.

To honor the third paradox—that the learning space invite the voices of both individual and group—I began by asking students to take a few minutes to reflect on the question in silence, the silence that most students require to think their best thoughts. Since simple silence is awkward for most people, I asked them to make notes as they reflected, giving them something to do. Then, in a subtle but shameless attempt to concentrate their minds on the task at hand, I said, "I will tell you in a minute what the notes are for."

Because my students did not know whether I would gather and grade their notes (which I would never do) or ask them to use their notes for personal reference in small groups (which I eventually did), all of them made notes, "just in case." Here is a small but significant flashback to the educative value of a charged ethos!

Then I made a gradual movement from the voice of the individual to the voice of the group. Following the personal reflection time, I asked students to gather for ten minutes in self-selected groups of three to share their reflections before the large group dialogue began. Small groups give everyone a chance to speak in a relatively safe setting, and the winnowing that they allow makes it more likely that students will have something of value to say when the large group discussion begins.

When the large group gathers, holding the tension of the third paradox—the voice of the individual and the voice of the group—depends heavily on the teacher's ability to facilitate rather than dictate the discussion. On one hand, the teacher must invite and affirm each individual's voice. That does not mean agreeing with everything that is said, no matter how ludicrous, as cynics sometimes suggest. It means helping each person find the best meaning in what he or she is saying by paying close attention, asking clarifying questions, and offering illustrations if the student gets lost in abstraction.

On the other hand, this paradox requires the teacher to give voice to whatever thought pattern may be emerging from the group: the group does not have a voice until the teacher gives it one. This means listening carefully and holding all the threads of the conversation in mind so that one can eventually lift up a fabric of thought and ask, "Does this look like what you have been saying?" I did this when I showed my students how the self-centeredness they claimed when questioned about their theory of freedom contrasted with the communal ethic they revealed when confronted with an actual dilemma.

The fourth paradox—that we must honor both the little stories of our lives and the big stories of the disciplines—is woven into all the pedagogical moves I have described. It is a hard tension to hold—not only because academia discredits the little story but also because the little stories are the ones students feel most comfortable with. Given free rein, they will hide out in their little stories and evade the big ones.

Though our little stories contain truths that can check and correct the big story (as my students' Appalachian experience corrected the big story in *Habits of the Heart*), the teacher must keep using the big story to reframe the little ones. I did this when I used concepts from *Habits* to point out that my students' resistance to suing the police for false arrest revealed a stronger communal ethic than their talk about freedom had suggested.

The key to holding this paradox is the knowledge that though students can tell their own stories, they, like the rest of us, rarely understand the meanings of the stories they tell. How could they, when education so seldom treats their lives as sources of knowledge? The teacher who wants to teach at the intersection of all the stories, big and little, must continually make interpretations that students do not know how to make—until they have been "heard to speech" often enough to do it for themselves.

The fifth paradox—that the space should support solitude and surround it with the resources of community—is usually implemented only in a metaphorical sense. In most educational settings, we cannot send students off for solitary reflection in the middle of class. But what we can do, even as we are developing a collective voice around a given issue, is to honor the soul's need for solitude within the group.

For example, I tell my students that much as I value dialogue, I affirm their right not to participate overtly in the conversation—as long as I have the sense, and occasional verbal reassurance, that they are participating inwardly. This permission *not* to speak seems to evoke speech from people who are normally silent: we are more likely to choose participation when we are granted the freedom to do so.

Honoring the solitude of my students' souls also means that as I listen to them speak, I must discern how deeply to draw them into a topic with my questions. There are some places where the human soul does not want to go—not, at least, in full view of other people.

I came to such a moment in case one when that young man told the story of his false arrest. I knew immediately the question I wanted to ask him, a question that would raise the issue of freedom versus accountability that had yet to surface in our discussion: "Why didn't you sue the police for false arrest? You might have gotten rich overnight."

But that question has sharp edges, especially in a context of poverty. It could easily be heard as "What are you—stupid? You blew a chance to get rich." So before I could ask the question, I needed to ask myself: Can this student handle the question? Do he and I have the kind of relationship that would keep him from being wounded? This is the metaphorical meaning of protecting a student's solitude: inviting the whole truth while refusing to violate the vulnerability of his or her soul.

The sixth paradox involves creating a space that welcomes both silence and speech. In the session I am examining, there was much talk but only one clear period of silence—when I asked students to collect their thoughts and make notes on the questions I had posed. That was a valuable interlude. But the silences that interest me most are the ones that occur midstream in a discussion, when a point is made or a question is posed that evokes no immediate response.

As the seconds tick by and the silence deepens, my belief in the value of silence goes on trial. Like most people, I am conditioned to interpret silence as a symptom of something gone wrong. I am the salaried leader of this classroom enterprise, and I live by an ethic of professional responsibility, so in the silence my sense of competence and worth is at stake: I am the one who must set right what has gone wrong—by speaking. Panic catapults me to the conclusion that the point just made or the question just raised has left students either dumbfounded or bored, and I am duty-bound to apply conversational CPR.

But suppose that my panic has misled me and my quick conclusion is mistaken. Suppose that my students are neither dumbfounded nor dismissive but digging deep; suppose that they are not ignorant or cynical but wise enough to know that this moment calls for thought; suppose that they are not wasting time but doing a more reflective form of learning. I miss all such possibilities when I assume that their silence signifies a problem, reacting to it from my own need for control rather than their need to learn.

Even if my hopeful interpretations are mistaken, it is indisputable that the moment I break the silence, I foreclose on all chances for authentic learning. Why would my students think their own thoughts in the silence when they know I will invariably fill it with thoughts of my own?

The particular way of practicing paradox I have just described may have more to do with my identity than with yours. But practicing paradox in the classroom is not unique to the kinds of subjects or students I teach.

I have been in high school science labs where the paradox of the individual and group voice is honored as students look into microscopes, one by one, then gather to seek consensus on what they have seen and what it means. I know teachers of grade school mathematics who understand that the charge of math's mysteries must be held in paradox with an ethos of hospitality, especially if girls and minority youngsters are to overcome a culture that says they are less capable of quantitative thinking. I have visited college literature courses where the big story and the little stories are held in paradoxical tension as the teacher helps students understand the drama of the family in *King Lear* by relating it to family dramas that the students know firsthand.

The principle of paradox offers no cookbook fix for teaching. But if it fits who you are, it offers guidance on any level of education and with any field of study.

HOLDING THE TENSION OF OPPOSITES

Holding the tension of paradox so that our students can learn at deeper levels is among the most difficult demands of good teaching. How are we supposed to do it?

Imagine yourself in a classroom. You ask a well-framed question, and then you wait and wait as the great silence descends. You know you should wait some more, not jump, but your heart pounds, then sinks, and finally feels helpless and out of control. So you answer your own question with an emotional mix of anxiety, anger, and authoritarianism that only makes things worse. Then you watch as the opening to learning offered by the silence vanishes—and teaching becomes more and more like running headlong into walls.

That scenario—which could apply to holding any of the paradoxes, not just silence and speech—suggests a simple truth: the place where paradoxes are held together is in the teacher's heart, and our inability to hold them is less a failure of technique than a gap in our inner lives. If we want to teach and learn in the power of paradox, we must reeducate our hearts.

In particular, we must teach our hearts a new way to understand the tension we feel when we are torn between the poles. Some clues to such an understanding are found in E. F. Schumacher's classic text, *Small Is Beautiful:*

The Hidden Wholeness

Through all our lives we are faced with the task of reconciling opposites which, in logical thought, cannot be reconciled. . . . How can one reconcile the demands of freedom and discipline in education? Countless mothers and teachers, in fact, do it, but no one can write down a solution. They do it by bringing into the situation a force that belongs to a higher level where opposites are transcended—the power of love. . . . Divergent problems, as it were, force us to strain ourselves to a level above ourselves; they demand, and thus provoke the supply of, forces from a higher level, thus bringing love, beauty, goodness and truth into our lives. It is only with the help of these higher forces that the opposites can be reconciled in the living situation.[5]

Schumacher's words help me understand that the tension that comes when I try to hold a paradox together is not hell-bent on tearing me apart. Instead, it is a power that wants to pull my heart open to something larger than myself. The tension always feels difficult, sometimes destructive. But if I can collaborate with the work it is trying to do rather than resist it, the tension will not break my heart—it will make my heart larger.

Schumacher's illustration of this point is brilliant because it is true to ordinary experience: every good teacher and every good parent has somehow learned to negotiate the paradox of freedom and discipline. We want our children and our students to become people who think and live freely, yet at the same time we know that helping them become free requires us to restrict their freedom in certain situations.

Of course, neither our children nor our students share this knowledge! When my thirteen-year-old announces that he will no longer attend religious services or a student submits a paper on a topic other than the one I assigned, I am immediately drawn into the tension—and there is no formula to tell me whether this is a moment for freedom or discipline or some alchemy of both.

But good teachers and good parents find their way through such minefields every day by allowing the tension itself to pull them open to a larger and larger love—a love that resolves these Solomonic dilemmas by looking past the tension within ourselves toward the best interests of the student or the child.

As always with profound truths, there is a paradox about this love. Schumacher says that a good parent or teacher resolves the tension of divergent problems by embodying the transcendent power of love. Yet he also says that resolving the tension requires a supply of love that comes from beyond ourselves, provoked by the tension itself. If we are to hold paradoxes together, our own love is absolutely necessary—and yet our own love is never enough. In a time of tension, we must endure with whatever love we can muster until that very tension draws a larger love into the scene.

There is a name for the endurance we must practice until a larger love arrives: it is called suffering. We will not be able to teach in the power of paradox until we are willing to suffer the tension of opposites, until we understand that such suffering is neither to be avoided nor merely to be survived but must be actively embraced for the way it expands our own hearts.

Without this acceptance, the pain of suffering will always lead us to resolve the tension prematurely, because we have no reason to stand the gaff. We will ask and answer our own questions in the silence of the classroom (thus creating more silence); we will ride roughshod over the dissenting voice that confounds our learning plan (even though we said we welcomed questions); we will punish the student who writes outside the assignment (no matter how creatively) to bring him or her back in line.

We cannot teach our students at the deepest levels when we are unable to bear the suffering that opens into those levels. By holding the tension of opposites, we hold the gateway to inquiry open, inviting students into a territory in which we all can learn.

How to do this is not a question that can be answered, for it is done in the teacher's heart: holding the tension of opposites is about being, not doing. But some words from Rilke may help. They offer no technique for embracing suffering, because one does not exist. But they offer hope for what might happen if we tried.

The words are from *Letters to a Young Poet,* in which Rilke writes as a teacher. He had received a series of respectful but demanding letters from a neophyte who admired Rilke's work and sought advice on how to follow in his path. Rilke not only took the time to respond but did so with astonishing generosity.

In one exchange, the young poet presses the older one with question after urgent question, and Rilke replies with this counsel: "Be patient toward all that is unsolved in your heart and try to love the *questions themselves*. . . . Do not now seek the answers, which cannot be given you because you would not be able to live them. And the point is, to live everything. *Live* the questions now. Perhaps you will then gradually, without noticing it, live along some distant day into the answer."[6]

His words could easily be paraphrased to speak to the condition of the teacher whose heart is unable to hold the tension of opposites in the classroom: Be patient toward all that is unresolved in your heart. . . . Try to love the contradictions themselves. . . . Do not now seek the resolutions, which cannot be given because you would not be able to live them—and the point is to live everything. Live the contradictions now. Perhaps you will then gradually, without noticing it, live along some distant day into the paradox.

The hope Rilke gives me lies partly in his notion that on "some distant day" I might find that I have lived my way into a more confident understanding of how to hold the tension of paradox than I have at this moment. Surely he is right about that: having lived into the tensions of teaching for some time now, I am better able to hold paradoxes together than I was years ago.

But my deeper hope comes with Rilke's words "and the point is to live everything." Of course that is the point! If I do not fully live the tensions that come my way, those tensions do not disappear: they go underground and multiply. I may not know how to solve them, but by wrapping my life around them and trying to live out their resolution, I open myself to new possibilities and keep the tensions from tearing me apart.

There is only one alternative: an unlived life, a life lived in denial of the tensions that teaching brings. Here, I play a masked professional role, pretending outwardly that I have no tensions at all while inwardly all those tensions I pretend not to have are ripping the fabric of my life.

Pretending is another name for dividedness, a state that keeps us from cultivating the capacity for connectedness on which good teaching depends. When we pretend, we fall out of community with ourselves, our students, and the world around us, out of communion

THE COURAGE TO TEACH

with the common center that is both the root and the fruit of teaching at its best. But when we understand that "the point is to live everything," we will recover all that is lost.

I give the last word on this subject to Florida Scott-Maxwell, who, writing toward the end of a long and well-lived life, speaks with authority: "Some uncomprehended law holds us at a point of contradiction where we have no choice, where we do not like that which we love, where good and bad are inseparable partners impossible to tell apart, and where we—heart-broken and ecstatic—can only resolve the conflict by blindly taking it into our hearts. This used to be called being in the hands of God. Has anyone any better words to describe it?"[7]

Chapter IV

Knowing in Community

Joined by the Grace of Great Things

Whoever you are, no matter how lonely,
the world offers itself to your imagination,
calls to you like the wild geese, harsh and exciting—
over and over announcing your place
in the family of things.

—MARY OLIVER, "WILD GEESE"[1]

IMAGES OF COMMUNITY

For three chapters, we have been traversing the inner landscape of teaching and learning. We have surveyed some inner forces that disconnect us from our students, our subjects, and ourselves, and we have explored some inner practices that can help us bridge those gaps: reclaiming selfhood, confronting fear, and thinking the world together by means of paradox.

In this chapter and the next two, we turn toward community— the kind of community that teaching and learning require, that can help renew and express the capacity for connectedness at the heart of authentic education. As we move from the teacher's inner life to community in education, it may seem that the subject is changing, but it is not. The first three chapters were about cultivating the inner ground from which community grows; the next three are about growing community from that inner ground into the classroom and the larger world.

Community cannot take root in a divided life. Long before community assumes external shape and form, it must be present as seed in the undivided self: only as we are in communion with ourselves can we find community with others. Community is an outward and visible sign of an inward and invisible grace, the flowing of personal identity and integrity into the world of relationships. It is the same agenda of connectedness I have been exploring all along, writ large in the external world.

Here and in the next two chapters, I explore several models of community in education with one crucial question in mind: Do these models enhance and advance the educational mission of knowing, teaching, and learning? I am guided in this inquiry by an image of teaching that has challenged me for years, one that has an essential but seldom-named form of community at its core: *to teach is to create a space in which the community of truth is practiced.*

To clear a path toward the community of truth, I need to hack away some underbrush. Models of community (if not the thing itself) have grown like weeds in our society, a response to our deepening pain of disconnection and yearning "not to be cut off." I will look briefly at three that are prominent in our discussion these days—the therapeutic, civic, and marketing models—in hopes of shedding some light on the kind of community that education requires.

The therapeutic is the model most often implied when we use the word *community.* This model makes intimacy the highest value in human relationships, because intimacy is regarded as the best therapy for the pain of disconnection. An intimate relationship goes beyond an implicit capacity for connectedness: in intimacy, we explicitly share our deeper natures with each other, in the belief that we can be fully known and the trust that we will be fully accepted. At its best, therapeutic community is characterized by one of the many forms of love: between spouses and lovers, between parent and child, between good friends.

The therapeutic motif has a place in education simply because any loveless enterprise is likely to be pathological: it is hard to imagine a healthy school that lacks any trace of love for learning or for learners. I know of one college with a marvelous motto, "The pursuit of truth in the company of friends."[2] Its founders clearly understood that the rigors of that pursuit require a bond of affection between members of the expeditionary team.

But conventional applications of therapeutic community to education are neither as subtle nor as apt as that motto. On the contrary, they threaten teaching and learning with the assumption that intimacy is the best and most important thing that can happen between people—an assumption that sometimes becomes shrill and insistent, manifesting itself in the pseudo-communal ethos of "share or die!" sometimes found in the human potential movement.

Of course, we cannot demand intimacy of each other—and when we try, we only drive each other off, as many failed communal experiments have shown. But the educational liabilities of the therapeutic model run deeper still: when all our relationships are judged by the norm of intimacy, our world shrinks to a vanishing point.

Most of us will achieve genuine intimacy with only a handful of people in a lifetime. If being in community equals being intimate, a vast range of others and otherness falls beyond our reach. When intimacy becomes the norm, we lose our capacity for connectedness with the strange and the stranger that is at the heart of being educated. We lose our capacity to entertain people and ideas that are alien to what we think and who we are. The therapeutic model exploits our fear of otherness by reducing community to whatever can take familial or friendly form.

As a middle-class North American, I am unlikely to have an intimate relation to the poor or to the experience of poverty, but it is crucial that I feel my accountability for the poor and their plight. I am unlikely to have an intimate bond with the people of the Amazon basin and their ravaged rain forests, but it is crucial that I understand my ecological interdependence with them and their habitat. As an amateur in science, I am unlikely to be on intimate terms with people who propound the strange constructs of quantum mechanics, but it is crucial that I understand how they are reshaping the world of thought in which I live.

When we reject that with which we cannot become intimate, our lives are diminished. We need a standard more encompassing than intimacy by which to affirm that a relationship—with people, nature, or ideas—has meaning. Teaching and learning are undermined when therapeutic community becomes the norm in education.

The civic model of community offers an important corrective to the therapeutic. Here, the norm is not a narrow band of intimate encounters but rather the wide range of relations among strangers that make for a healthy body politic. The community envisioned by the civic model is one of public mutuality rather than personal vulnerability—a community where people who do not and cannot experience intimacy with each other nonetheless learn to share a common territory and common resources, to resolve mutual conflicts and mutual problems. In civic community, we may not learn what is on each others' hearts, but we learn that if we do not hang together, we will hang separately.

Therapeutic community is a modern concept, an artifact of the psychological age, but civic community grows from ancient roots. From Plato onward, the academy has been promoted as a microcosm of the body politic, a setting in which the habits of democratic citizenship can and should be cultivated. As Benjamin Barber has written, "This argument suggests not that the university *has* a civic mission, but that the university *is* a civic mission, is civility itself, defined as the rules or conventions that permit a community to facilitate conversation and the kinds of discourse on which all knowledge depends. . . . I mean to suggest much more than that democracy and education are parallel activities, or that civic training and the cultivation of knowledge and judgment possess a parallel structure. I am arguing that they are the same thing."[3]

The civic model of community has features vital to teaching and learning. In a society divided by race and ethnicity and gender, I am often moved by the fact that high school and college classrooms contain a broader cross section of people engaged in common work—and often doing it with civility, media-fueled "political correctness" wars notwithstanding—than one can find in many settings. As we reweave our tattered civic fabric, educational institutions are among our most important looms.

But the civic model also contains a subtle threat to education's core mission. In civic society, we deal with differences through the classic mechanisms of democratic politics—negotiation, bargaining, compromise. These are honorable arts in the civic arena, where the goal is the greatest good for the greatest number. But what is noble in a quest for the common good may be ignoble in a quest for truth: truth is not determined by democratic means.

In a democratic society we agree that once the ballots are counted, whoever or whatever receives the highest vote is the leader or the law of the land—and within the bounds of conscience, we

THE COURAGE TO TEACH

agree to follow. But in the quest for truth we make no such agreement, nor should we, for truth by majority rule is no truth at all. One sure way to miss truth in any field is to count the votes: had Copernicus and Galileo done so, the sun might still be circling the earth. For all the rightful claims that the civic model makes on teaching and learning, community in education must find a more fundamental form.

The marketing model of community is blitzing American education today under the flag of Total Quality Management. Though its aims and rationale are quite different from the models we have explored, it combines, in a curious way, the personalism of the therapeutic with the pragmatism of the civic.

The norms of the marketing model are straightforward: educational institutions must improve their product by strengthening relations with customers and becoming more accountable to them. Bill-paying students and parents must be treated as the consumers that they are and given ample opportunity to criticize their purchases. These criticisms must be passed on to the people who produce the product to help them change the way we educate people and satisfy more customers.

If you are an educator who finds talk of "customers" and "products" grating, here is a story that may speak to your condition. The new provost of a public university was talking about the weak community bonds on his large urban commuter campus. I asked, "If you could wave a magic wand, what is the first thing you would do to strengthen the sense of community here?" expecting him to talk about orientation or dorm life or counseling.

He responded, "I'd create some meaningful way to measure student reactions to the courses they are taking, and I'd use that information to help inadequate teachers get better. And if they were unable or unwilling to improve, I would help them find a different job."

The provost's concept of community may lack the psychological depth of the therapeutic model and the political nobility of the civic model, but it still has much to commend it. Whereas business is disciplined to some extent by market response, higher education has stayed aloof from its consumers. Bill-paying students and parents are often treated by academics with *lèse majesté*: we believe that no one except our peers can adequately judge our work—and we are not entirely sure about them!

In the face of that arrogance, the provost's concept of community might bring some humility to higher education, assuming that he, with the help of that magic wand, could create an evaluation system able to discern the subtleties and varieties of good teaching. But there are clear threats to teaching and learning in this version of the marketing model.

First, the evaluation system that the provost needs is nowhere in sight—and what stands in its place is a dangerous impostor. We lack reliable mechanisms for evaluating teaching, unless one believes that all varieties of good teaching can be crammed into the scales of a survey questionnaire.

Second, good education is always more process than product. If a student has received no more than a packet of information at the end of an educational transaction, that student has been duped. Good education teaches students to become both producers of knowledge and discerning consumers of what other people claim to know.

Third, good education may leave students deeply dissatisfied, at least for a while. I do not mean the dissatisfaction that comes from teachers who are inaudible, incoherent, or incompetent. But students who have been well served by good teachers may walk away angry—angry that their prejudices have been challenged and their sense of self shaken. That sort of dissatisfaction may be a sign that real education has happened.

It can take many years for a student to feel grateful to a teacher who introduces a dissatisfying truth. A marketing model of educational community, however apt its ethic of accountability, serves the cause poorly when it assumes that the customer is always right.

REALITY IS COMMUNAL

The therapeutic, civic, and marketing models of community contain insights that education needs. But the comprehensive form of community that supports authentic education is not on that list. In the remainder of this chapter, I offer an alternative model. In the two chapters that follow, I will explore its implications for practical pedagogy.

The model of community we seek is one that can embrace, guide, and refine the core mission of education—the mission of knowing, teaching, and learning. We will find clues to its dimensions at the heart of the image of teaching that most challenges me: to teach is to create a space in which the community of truth is practiced.

The hallmark of the community of truth is not psychological intimacy or political civility or pragmatic accountability, though it does not exclude these virtues. This model of community reaches deeper, into ontology and epistemology—into assumptions about the nature of reality and how we know it—on which all education is built. The hallmark of the community of truth is in its claim that *reality is a web of communal relationships, and we can know reality only by being in community with it.*

This is a large claim, but it can be illustrated by a small story. I was lecturing on community in education at a major research university. As I spoke, my eye was repeatedly drawn to a tall and deeply attentive listener near the front of the auditorium, a stately gentleman in his early seventies, impeccably dressed and crowned with a shock of theatrically white hair.

When our discussion began, this gentleman rose quickly and introduced himself: "I am Dr. Smith, Distinguished Such-and-Such Professor of Biology, Emeritus."

Knowing that academic savagery is sometimes preceded by mock courtliness and finding his self-introduction just a tad pompous, I drew a quick conclusion: he intends to have me for lunch—as an entrée, not a guest.

He continued, "I am not sure I understand all this fuss about community in higher education. After all, it's only good biology."

Then he sat down.

It took me a few seconds to realize that I had not been attacked but affirmed, albeit in the elliptical manner prescribed by academic etiquette. Once I understood that, the professor and I had a lively and informative exchange about the meaning of his remark.

Two or three generations ago, no professor of biology would have claimed that community was good science. On the contrary, the biologist of an earlier era would have mocked my case for educational community as a romantic fallacy that violated the cardinal principle of the discipline: life is a ceaseless round of warfare between individuals, a win-lose arena of combat and death. For that earlier generation of biologists, nature was, in Tennyson's famous phrase, "red in tooth and claw." For the Social Darwinists who built on that image of nature, human relations were no more than the survival of the fittest, thinly coated with a veneer of civilization.

But today, our images of biological reality have been transformed. Ecological studies offer a picture of nature less focused on the terrors of combat than on the dance of communal collaboration, a picture of the great web of being. Struggle and death have not disappeared from the natural world, but death is now understood as a factor in the ongoing life of the community rather than a failure in the life of the individual.

This transformation of images of reality—from fragmentation and competition to community and collaboration—has gone on in virtually every academic discipline over the past fifty years. Physics offers another example, powerful not only because physics is one of the revered "hard" sciences but also because physics portrays the most elemental levels of our material bodies and habitats.

From its inception, physics was shaped by the image of the atom, an image that originated in pre-Socratic philosophy, then took on new significance as modern physicists gained predictive, even political power by analyzing reality into its constituent parts. When the images of reductionist science merged with the modern experience of social alienation, "atomism" became the dominant cultural metaphor of our time: we and the world we live in are only an illusion of wholeness, beneath which lies the reality of fragmentation.

But the image of reality offered by recent physics renders this sort of atomism naive. In a series of critical experiments, physicists have shown that subatomic particles behave "as if there were some communication between them," even when they are "too far apart to communicate in the time available."[4] These so-called particles, widely separated in time and space, seem to be connected in ways that make them act less like isolated individuals and more like participants in an interactive and interdependent community.

Communal metaphors come readily to physicists trying to describe the world suggested by these experimental results. Paul Davies says that they point "to a surprisingly integrationist view of the relationship of systems which have once interacted with each other, however widely they may subsequently separate."[5] Henry Stapp says, even more decisively, "An elementary particle is not an independently-

THE COURAGE TO TEACH

existing, unanalyzable entity. It is, in essence, a set of relationships that reach outward to other things."[6]

When physicists go beyond description to ask why these particles behave in ways that are more relational than autonomous, the communal metaphors multiply. David Bohm has suggested that physical reality, much like the human genome, is made up of an invisible web of information, an incredibly complex community of coded messages, "a holistic underlying *implicate order* whose information unfolds into the explicate order of particular fields and particles. One analogy . . . is a holographic photograph, of which every part has three-dimensional information about the whole object photographed. If you cut the hologram into small pieces, you can unfold the whole image by illuminating any piece of it with laser light."[7]

Ian Barbour, a leading interpreter of modern science, offers a useful sketch of the stages that our images of reality have moved through on their way to naming "community" as the essential character of the physical world. In the medieval era, we saw reality as mental and material substance, or "stuff." In the Newtonian era, our image was atomistic, "taking separate particles rather than substances to be the basic nature of reality."[8]

But in our era, "nature is understood to be relational, ecological, and interdependent. Reality is constituted by events and relationships rather than separate substances or separate particles." According to Barbour, we are now compelled to see nature as a "historical community of interdependent beings."[9]

The first step toward understanding the community of truth is to understand that community is the essential form of reality, the matrix of all being. The next step takes us from the nature of reality to the question of how we know it: *we know reality only by being in community with it ourselves.*

Modern physics has debunked the notion that knowing requires, or even allows, a separation of the knower from the known. Physicists cannot study subatomic particles without altering them in the act of knowing, so we cannot maintain the objectivist gap between the world "out there" and the observer "in here" as posited by premodern science. Knower and known are joined, and any claim about the nature of the known reflects the nature of the knower as well.

In macroscopic fields, the symbiosis between knower and known seems obvious—especially once we have been freed from the myth that "real" science requires their separation. How can one human being know something about another, in sociology or psychology or history, without leaving the mark of the knowing self on the thing known? How can a literary critic stroll through the territory laid out in a novel without leaving the footprints of personal experience?

But the crucial, and often misunderstood, feature of relational knowing is that it turns our human capacity for connectedness into a strength. As knowers, we no longer need to regret our yearning to connect meaningfully with the other—nor do we need to "overcome" this "liability" by disconnecting ourselves from the world.

Now we can celebrate the fact that by virtue of being human, we are members of the cosmic community, quite literally: in the farthest reaches of space, astronomers have found exploding stars that are the original seedbeds of the atoms that make up your body and mine. If we were not so entwined with the cosmos, if we were here merely as observers and not participants in the world, we would have no capacity to know.

In his landmark book, *Personal Knowledge,* the chemist Michael Polanyi shows how science relies on the fact that we, by "indwelling" the world, are given "bodily knowledge" of it—an inarticulate and "tacit" form of knowledge on which our explicit and articulate knowledge depends.[10]

Without tacit knowledge, scientists would be clueless about where to turn for revealing questions, for promising hypotheses, for fruitful intuitions and insights about the direction in which truth may lie. The clues that allow us to know anything come from our relatedness to reality—a relatedness as deep as the atoms our bodies share with everything that is, ever has been, or ever will be.

Richard Gelwick, an interpreter of Polanyi's thought, has pointed out that objectivism is taken so much for granted that Polanyi's insight about the personal element of knowing has often been misunderstood, even by his proponents:

> Several times in public lectures, I heard [Polanyi] correct people who stood up to support him, [people who said] that they agreed

that all knowledge had a personal element in it . . . [and] then went on to say that this personal element was the risky part and that we should try to minimize it. Polanyi would . . . explain that the personal was not to be minimized but understood as the element that was essential, the one that led us to break out and make new discoveries, and not at all an unfortunate imperfection in human epistemology. On the contrary, it is the cornerstone upon which culture, civilization, and progress were developed.[11]

The community of truth is an image of knowing that embraces both the great web of being on which all things depend and the fact that our knowing of those things is helped, not hindered, by our being enmeshed in that web. It is an image that lifts up not only our visible connections to human forms of being—with their opportunities for intimacy, civility, and accountability—but our invisible connections to nonhuman forms as well. It is a model of community capacious enough to carry the educational mission of knowing, teaching, and learning.

TRUTH REVISITED

Truth is not a word much spoken in educational circles these days. It suggests an earlier, more naive era when people were confident they could know the truth. But we are confident we cannot, so we refuse to use the word for fear of embarrassing ourselves.

Of course, the fact that we do not use the word does not mean that we have freed ourselves from the concept, let alone the possibilities to which it points. On the contrary, the less we talk about truth, the more likely that our knowing, teaching, and learning will be dominated by a traditional—and mythical—model of truth, the objectivist model so deeply embedded in our collective unconscious that to ignore it is to give it power.

Because the community of truth is an alternative to this unconscious and mythical objectivism, it will be easier to describe my vision of educational community and how it works if I first raise the objectivist myth to visible form, which I do in Figure 4.1.

Knowing in Community

Figure 4.1. *The Objectivist Myth of Knowing.*

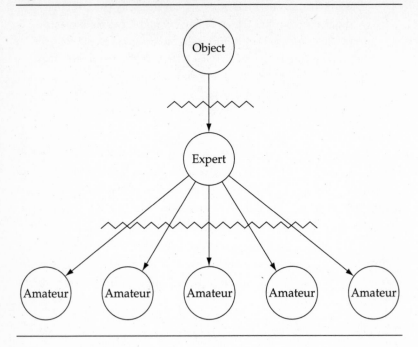

This mythical but dominant model of truth-knowing and truth-telling has four major elements:

1. *Objects* of knowledge that reside "out there" somewhere, pristine in physical or conceptual space, as described by the "facts" in a given field.

2. *Experts,* people trained to know these objects in their pristine form without allowing their own subjectivity to slop over onto the purity of the objects themselves. This training transpires in a far-off place called graduate school, whose purpose is so thoroughly to obliterate one's sense of self that one becomes a secular priest, a safe bearer of the pure objects of knowledge.

3. *Amateurs,* people without training and full of bias, who depend on the experts for objective or pure knowledge of the pristine objects in question.

THE COURAGE TO TEACH

4. *Baffles* at every point of transmission—between objects and experts, between experts and amateurs—that allow objective knowledge to flow downstream while preventing subjectivity from flowing back up.

The image of baffles came to me on overhearing a marvelous remark: "We don't seem to mind if civilization goes down the drain, as long as the drain doesn't back up!" Objectivism, obsessed with the purity of knowledge, wants to avoid the mess of subjectivity at all costs—even if the cost is the "decivilizing" kind of knowledge that renders us unfit for the messiness of life.

In the objectivist myth, truth flows from the top down, from experts who are qualified to know truth (including some who claim that truth is an illusion) to amateurs who are qualified only to receive truth. In this myth, truth is a set of propositions about objects; education is a system for delivering those propositions to students; and an educated person is one who can remember and repeat the experts' propositions. The image is hierarchical, linear, and compulsive-hygienic, as if truth came down an antiseptic conveyer belt to be deposited as pure product at the end.

There are only two problems with this myth: it falsely portrays how we know, and it has profoundly deformed the way we educate. I know a thousand classrooms where the relationships of teacher, students, and subject look exactly like this image. But I know of no field—from astronomy to literature to political science to theology—where the continuing quest to know truth even vaguely resembles this mythical objectivism.

The community of truth represents knowing quite differently (see Figure 4.2). In the community of truth, as in real life, there are no pristine objects of knowledge and no ultimate authorities. In the community of truth, as in real life, truth does not reside primarily in propositions, and education is more than delivering propositions about objects to passive auditors. In the community of truth, knowing and teaching and learning look less like General Motors and more like a town meeting, less like a bureaucracy and more like bedlam.

The community of truth is, in fact, many communities, far-flung across space and ever-changing through time. I name it with a

Figure 4.2. *The Community of Truth.*

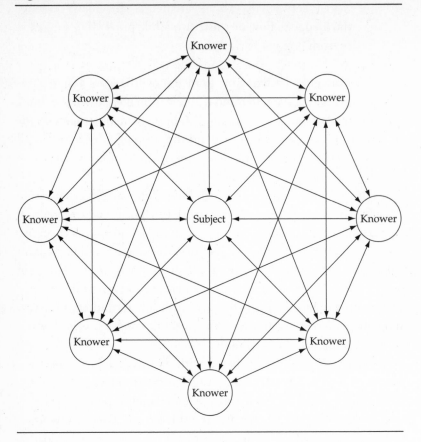

singular noun because in any given field, the many are made one by the fact that they gather around a common subject and are guided by shared rules of observation and interpretation that require them to approach the subject in the same way. Thus biologists in twentieth-century America and Linnaeus and his colleagues in eighteenth-century Sweden, despite their vast differences in theory and technique, are one, giving this form of community a longevity and reach that make it one of our most powerful social forms.

At the center of this communal circle, there is always a subject— as contrasted with the object at the top of the objectivist ladder. This distinction is crucial to knowing, teaching, and learning: *a subject is available for relationship; an object is not.* When we know the other as a subject, we do not merely hold it at arm's length. We know it in and through relationship, the kind of relationship Barbara McClintock had with the corn plants that she studied.

This relationship begins when we allow the subject to occupy the center of our attention, exactly as the diagram suggests. This contrasts sharply with objectivism, which puts the expert at the center of our attention: in objectivism, the objects of knowing are so far beyond our reach that the expert is the only party with whom we can connect.

When we make the subject the center of our attention, we give it the respect and authority that we normally give only to human beings. We give it ontological significance, the significance that Barbara McClintock gave to an ear of corn, acknowledging its unique identity and integrity.[12] In the community of truth, the connective core of all our relationships is the significant subject itself—not intimacy, not civility, not accountability, not the experts, but the power of the living subject.

As we try to understand the subject in the community of truth, we enter into complex patterns of communication—sharing observations and interpretations, correcting and complementing each other, torn by conflict in this moment and joined by consensus in the next. The community of truth, far from being linear and static and hierarchical, is circular, interactive, and dynamic.

At its best, the community of truth advances our knowledge through conflict, not competition. Competition is a secretive, zero-sum game played by individuals for private gain; conflict is open and sometimes raucous but always communal, a public encounter in which it is possible for everyone to win by learning and growing. Competition is the antithesis of community, an acid that can dissolve the fabric of relationships. Conflict is the dynamic by which we test ideas in the open, in a communal effort to stretch each other and make better sense of the world.

This communal dynamic is governed by rules of observation and interpretation that help define us as a community by bringing focus and discipline to our discourse. To be in the community of truth, we must abide by its norms and procedures, which differ from one field to another, from art history to chemistry to philosophy. These standards are strong but not chiseled in stone: they evolve,

Knowing in Community

even as our understanding of a subject evolves. We can challenge and change the norms, but we must be able to justify any deviation from them in a public and compelling way.

Implicit in this exploration of how we know is an image of truth that can now be made explicit: *truth is an eternal conversation about things that matter, conducted with passion and discipline.*

Unlike the objectivist, I do not understand truth to be lodged in the conclusions we reach about objects of knowledge. How could it be, since the conclusions keep changing? I understand truth as the passionate and disciplined process of inquiry and dialogue itself, as the dynamic conversation of a community that keeps testing old conclusions and coming into new ones.

We need to know the current conclusions in order to get in on the conversation. But it is not our knowledge of conclusions that keeps us in the truth. It is our commitment to the conversation itself, our willingness to put forward our observations and interpretations for testing by the community and to return the favor to others. To be in the truth, we must know how to observe and reflect and speak and listen, with passion and with discipline, in the circle gathered around a given subject.

If truth is an eternal conversation whose conclusions and norms keep changing, what happens to the idea of objective knowledge? I do not think that my image of truth alters anything about the nature of objectivity—except the objectivist myth.

As far as I can tell, the only "objective" knowledge we possess is the knowledge that comes from a community of people looking at a subject and debating their observations within a consensual framework of procedural rules. I know of no field, from science to religion, where what we regard as objective knowledge did not emerge from long and complex communal discourse that continues to this day, no field where the facts of the matter were delivered fully formed from on high.

The firmest foundation of all our knowledge is the community of truth itself. This community can never offer us ultimate certainty—not because its process is flawed but because certainty is beyond the grasp of finite hearts and minds. Yet this community can do much to rescue us from ignorance, bias, and self-deception if we are willing to submit our assumptions, our observations, our theories—indeed, ourselves—to its scrutiny.

In rejecting the objectivist model, I have not embraced a relativism that reduces truth to whatever the community decides, for the community of truth includes a transcendent dimension of truth-knowing and truth-telling that takes us beyond relativism and absolutism alike. The clearest and most compelling naming of that dimension is found in a couplet by Robert Frost: "We dance round in a ring and suppose,/But the Secret sits in the middle and knows."[13]

Frost honors the transcendent secret of the subject at the center of the community of truth, a secret that is equally obscured by absolutism, which claims that we can know the full reality of things, and by relativism, which claims that things have no reality save what we know. The subject knows itself better than we can ever know it, and it forever evades our grasp by keeping its own secrets.

If this were not the case, the process of knowing would have long ago come to a halt. Why did we not settle for the pre-Socratic view of the nature of the physical world or the medieval view or the view of early modern science? Why are we pressing, even now, on the view we hold today? Because at the center of our attention is a subject that continually calls us deeper into its secret, a subject that refuses to be reduced to our conclusions about it.

The idea of a subject that calls to us is more than metaphor. In the community of truth, the knower is not the only active agent—the subject itself participates in the dialectic of knowing. It is as Mary Oliver says: "The world offers itself to your imagination,/calls to you like the wild geese . . . ,/. . . announcing your place / in the family of things."[14]

We say that knowing begins in our intrigue about some subject, but that intrigue is the result of the subject's action upon us: geologists are people who hear rocks speak, historians are people who hear the voices of the long dead, writers are people who hear the music of words. The things of the world call to us, and we are drawn to them—each of us to different things, as each is drawn to different friends.

Once we have heard that call and responded, the subject calls us out of ourselves and into its own selfhood. At the deepest reaches, knowing requires us to imagine the inner standpoint of the subject—of that historical moment, of that literary character, of that rock, or of that ear of corn. As one research scientist has said, "If you want to really understand about a tumor, you've got to *be* a tumor."[15]

We cannot know the subject well if we stand only in our own shoes. We must believe in the subject's inner life and enter with empathy into it, an empathy unavailable to us when we neither believe in nor cultivate an inner life of our own. When we deny or disparage the knower's inner life, as is the objectivist habit, we have no capacity to intuit, let alone inhabit, the inwardness of the known.

The sort of science done by Barbara McClintock requires one to fathom the mystery of self in order to fathom the mystery of the world, to become—as a colleague said of McClintock—"someone who understands where the mysteries lie" rather "than someone who mystifies."[16]

As we gather around the subject in the community of truth, it is not only we who correct each other's attempts at knowing, rejecting blurry observations and false interpretations. The subject itself corrects us, resisting our false framings with the strength of its own identity, refusing to be reduced to our self-certain ways of naming its otherness.

Eventually, as our insight deepens, the subject yields to a certain naming, and we conclude that we know it. But the transcendent subject always stands ready to take us by surprise, calling us into new observations, interpretations, and namings and into the mystery that can never be fully named.

Openness to transcendence is what distinguishes the community of truth from both absolutism and relativism. In this community, the process of truth-knowing and truth-telling is neither dictatorial nor anarchic. Instead, it is a complex and eternal dance of intimacy and distance, of speaking and listening, of knowing and not knowing, that makes collaborators and co-conspirators of the knowers and the known.

THE GRACE OF GREAT THINGS

The community of truth is an image that can carry the educational mission because it embraces an essential fact: the reality we belong to, the reality we long to know, extends far beyond human beings interacting with one another. In the community of truth, we interact with nonhuman forms of being that are as important and powerful as the human and sometimes even more so. This is a community held together not only by our personal powers of thought and feeling but also by the power of "the grace of great things."[17]

That phrase comes from an essay by Rilke. When I read it, I realized that our conventional images of educational community ignore our relationships with the great things that call us together—the things that call us to know, to teach, to learn. I saw how diminished the educational community becomes when it excludes the grace of great things and relies entirely on our own quite limited graces.

By *great things,* I mean the subjects around which the circle of seekers has always gathered—not the disciplines that study these subjects, not the texts that talk about them, not the theories that explain them, but the things themselves.

I mean the genes and ecosystems of biology, the symbols and referents of philosophy and theology, the archetypes of betrayal and forgiveness and loving and loss that are the stuff of literature. I mean the artifacts and lineages of anthropology, the materials of engineering with their limits and potentials, the logic of systems in management, the shapes and colors of music and art, the novelties and patterns of history, the elusive idea of justice under law.

Great things such as these are the vital nexus of community in education. It is in the act of gathering around them and trying to understand them—as the first humans must have gathered around fire—that we become who we are as knowers, teachers, and learners. When we are at our best, it is because the grace of great things has evoked from us the virtues that give educational community its finest form:

- We invite *diversity* into our community not because it is politically correct but because diverse viewpoints are demanded by the manifold mysteries of great things.

- We embrace *ambiguity* not because we are confused or indecisive but because we understand the inadequacy of our concepts to embrace the vastness of great things.

- We welcome *creative conflict* not because we are angry or hostile but because conflict is required to correct our biases and prejudices about the nature of great things.

Knowing in Community

- We practice *honesty* not only because we owe it to one another but because to lie about what we have seen would be to betray the truth of great things.
- We experience *humility* not because we have fought and lost but because humility is the only lens through which great things can be seen—and once we have seen them, humility is the only posture possible.
- We become *free* men and women through education not because we have privileged information but because tyranny in any form can be overcome only by invoking the grace of great things.

Of course, the educational community is not always at its best! We can easily cite instances when the community of truth has been driven by the antithesis of virtues such as these. *The Double Helix* is a book that chronicles such a case: the discovery of DNA by James Watson and Francis Crick, a case in which ego and competition, pigheadedness and greed, are shown to lie at the heart of the academic enterprise.[18]

So it intrigues me that the two principals in that story, interviewed on the fortieth anniversary of their discovery, spoke about the way certain virtues have overtaken them since they first encountered the great thing called DNA.

James Watson said, "The molecule is so beautiful. Its glory was reflected on Francis and me. I guess the rest of my life has been spent trying to prove that I was almost equal to being associated with DNA, which has been a hard task."

Then Francis Crick—of whom Watson once said, "I have never seen him in a modest mood"—replied, "We were upstaged by a molecule."[19]

Crick's humility may be uncharacteristic and strained, but that only makes it a more compelling example of the power of the community of truth—a community in which even our own agendas are sometimes upstaged by the grace of great things. When the great things disappear, when they lose their gravitational pull on our lives, we fall out of the communal orbit into the black hole of posturing, narcissism, and arrogance.

How do the great things disappear? They dim, if they do not disappear altogether, when the image of community that forms (or deforms) education has more to do with intimacy, majority rule, or marketing than with knowing, teaching, and learning. But there is a deeper threat to great things: they are killed off by an intellectual arrogance that tries to reduce them to nothing more than the machinations of our minds.

The great things disappear in the face of both absolutism and relativism. With absolutism, we claim to know precisely the nature of great things, so there is no need to continue in dialogue with them—or with each other. The experts possess the facts, and all that remains is for them to transmit those facts to those who do not know. With relativism, we claim that knowledge depends wholly on where one stands, so we cannot know anything with any certainty beyond our personal point of view. Once again, there is no need to continue in dialogue with great things or with each other: one truth for you, another for me, and never mind the difference.

Of course, the great things do not disappear in reality—they only disappear from our view. The great things themselves survive all the assaults of human arrogance, for they are the irreducible elements of life itself and of the life of the mind. The question is, will we abandon the arrogance that claims either to know the world perfectly or to invent the world at will? Will we acknowledge the independent reality of great things and their power to work on our lives?

We will experience the power of great things only when we grant them a life of their own—an inwardness, identity, and integrity that make them more than objects, a quality of being and agency that does not rely on us and our thoughts about them.

To understand this more fully, we need only look at what happens when we rob great things of their integrity. In the study of literature, it is now common to teach classic texts through analytical lenses that show how riddled they are with the biases of their authors and their times. From this standpoint, it does not matter that *Moby Dick* reaches deep into such great things in the human experience as hubris and destiny. It matters only that Melville was a patriarchal bigot.

David Denby has shown the hubris of this posture itself: it gives us, teachers and students alike, feelings of superiority to the text, thereby depriving us of the chance to learn anything from it except how superior we are.[20] It is impossible to be in a learning relationship with a text or a person that one regards as morally bankrupt. When we reduce great things to such dismissive categories, we rob them of their selfhood and deprive them of their voice.

It is not cheap mysticism to claim that all great things have inner lives that will speak to our own—if we let them. Literary texts are merely the clearest example of such voices, voices that reach us with astonishing clarity across huge gaps of space and time. The history of the Third Reich speaks a voice of evil that if I listen carefully to it, will find echoes in my own soul.

A marine biologist can pick up a seashell and, through careful listening, learn much about what happened in the lifetime of its inhabitant and in the evolution of its species. Every geologist knows that even the rocks speak, telling tales across gaps of time far wider than recorded history, stories we would not know if human vocalization were the only speech we could hear.

Annie Dillard titled one of her books *Teaching a Stone to Talk*, but the real issue, as Dillard knows, is teaching ourselves to listen.[21] The inner life of any great thing will be incomprehensible to me until I develop and deepen an inner life of my own. I cannot know in another being what I do not know in myself.

The conclusion seems clear: we cannot know the great things of the universe until we know ourselves to be great things. Absolutism and relativism have ravaged not only the things of the world but our sense of the knowing self as well. We are whiplashed between an arrogant overestimation of ourselves and a servile underestimation of ourselves, but the outcome is always the same: a distortion of the humble yet exalted reality of the human self, a paradoxical pearl of great price.

I once heard this Hasidic tale: "We need a coat with two pockets. In one pocket there is dust, and in the other pocket there is gold. We need a coat with two pockets to remind us who we are."[22] Knowing, teaching, and learning under the grace of great things will come from teachers who own such a coat and who wear it to class every day.

KNOWING AND THE SACRED

The images of knowing central to this chapter—the community of truth, the grace of great things, the transcendent subject, the "Secret" that "sits in the middle and knows"—these images emerge, for me, from my experience of reality as sacred and of the sacred as real. Others may arrive at similar understandings from different starting points. But I believe that knowing, teaching, and learning are grounded in sacred soil and that renewing my vocation as a teacher requires cultivating a sense of the sacred.

I am well aware that the marriage of knowing and the sacred has not always produced admirable offspring. But the history of education will show that spirituality is no worse than secularism in its propensity to sow bad seed. I know of no religious pathology, from fear to bigotry to rigid orthodoxy, that is not also found in secular form, comfortably ensconced in the groves of academe. The health of education depends on our ability to hold sacred and secular together so that they can correct and enrich each other.

What do I mean by *sacred*? It is a paradoxical concept—as one would expect when exploring the most profound truth of all. On one hand, the word points to an ineffable immensity beyond concept and definition, the sacred as Rudolf Otto defined it in *The Idea of the Holy*—the *mysterium tremendum,* the numinous energy at the heart of reality.[23] On the other hand, sacred means, quite simply, "worthy of respect." Access to the *mysterium tremendum* is not a staple of my daily experience, so I cannot depend on a steady stream of numinosity to renew my teaching. But I can practice continuous respect for the great things of the world.

Many critics have noted the growing disrespect inherent in our social relations and the sad implications of such incivility for the future of democracy. But fewer have noticed our growing disrespect for the "grace of great things" and its sad implications for the future of teaching and learning and the life of the mind.

In a culture of disrespect, education suffers the worst possible fate—it becomes banal. When nothing is sacred, deemed worthy of respect, banality is the best we can do. What could be more banal than to stand in the midst of this astonishing universe, sifting its wonders through reductionist screens, debunking amazement with data and logic, downsizing mystery to the scale of our own minds? The root of all banality—including, as Hannah Arendt named it, "the banality of evil"—is our failure to find the other worthy of respect.[24]

In a world stripped of the sacred, the inner landscape holds no mystery, for it has no variety. Traveling through it, one does not move from prairie to woods to water, from desert to mountain to valley, from the plotted and cultivated to the primal and wild. The desacralized landscape is utterly flat, bereft of texture and tangle, color and flair—and traversing it soon becomes tedious beyond telling.

If this were only an aesthetic failure, it would be bad enough. But the flatness of the desacralized landscape breeds more than sensory fatigue. It creates a specific spiritual pathology that diminishes our ability to know, to teach, to learn: we lose our capacity for surprise.

In a sacred landscape, with its complexities and convolutions, surprise is a constant companion: it lies just around the bend or hidden in the next valley, and though it sometimes startles us, it often brings delight. But on the flatlands of a desacralized world, where we grow accustomed to seeing things approaching us long before they arrive, surprise is neither expected nor welcomed. When it suddenly arises, apparently out of nowhere, we are stricken with fear and may even respond with violence.

This is what happens in academic culture when we are surprised by a new idea that does not fit our conventional frame—for example, the pedagogical insight that feelings are as important as facts or Barbara McClintock's scientific hypothesis that genes "jump" or are transposable.

We do not always welcome such novel notions. Instead, we swat them away as irritating nonsense; depending on the stakes, we may even try to destroy them, as if they were enemies on the battlefield trying to gain strategic advantage. The geneticist James Shapiro summarizes this pattern of resistance nicely: McClintock's news of transposable elements, he points out, is "an example of how new ideas are accepted coldly by the scientific community." When McClintock first announced the phenomenon, people called her crazy; "then they said it's peculiar to maize; then they said it's everywhere but has no significance; and then finally they woke up to its significance."[25]

It is possible to respond differently to surprises, to allow one new idea to generate yet another in us—a process sometimes called thinking. But in a flattened, desacralized culture, thinking is not what happens when we are taken—or threatened—by surprise. Instead, we reflexively defend ourselves by reaching for a weapon that we know how to use, an old idea whose use we mastered long ago.

To think a new thought in this moment of danger would leave us open and vulnerable, for we do not know what flank it might leave exposed. So we grab an old idea, a conceptual club we know how to use because we have swung it many times before, and we beat the surprise to death—or we run away before it can make a mark on our minds. Startled by otherness, reacting out of fear, we destroy the possibility of learning anything new by allowing the ancient fight or flight syndrome to have its way.

This reflex is rooted in a million years of evolution, so it may seem inexorable. Yet there is some physiological evidence that this need not be the case.[26] Normally, when we are taken by surprise, there is a sudden narrowing of our visual periphery that exacerbates the fight or flight response—an intense, fearful, self-defensive focusing of the "gimlet eye" that is associated with both physical and intellectual combat. But in the Japanese self-defense art of aikido, this visual narrowing is countered by a practice called "soft eyes," in which one learns to widen one's periphery, to take in more of the world.

If you introduce a sudden stimulus to an unprepared person, the eyes narrow and the fight or flight syndrome kicks in. But if you train a person to practice soft eyes, then introduce that same stimulus, the reflex is often transcended. This person will turn toward the stimulus, take it in, and then make a more authentic response—such as thinking a new thought.

Soft eyes, it seems to me, is an evocative image for what happens when we gaze on sacred reality. Now our eyes are open and receptive, able to take in the greatness of the world and the grace of great things. Eyes wide with wonder, we no longer need to resist or run when taken by surprise. Now we can open ourselves to the great mystery. Now we can invite our students into the great affair that Diane Ackerman writes about, the affair called living and learning: "The great affair, the love affair with life, is to live as variously as possible, to groom one's curiosity like a high-spirited thoroughbred, climb aboard, and gallop over the thick, sun-struck hills every day. Where there is no risk, the emotional terrain is flat and unyielding, and, despite all its dimensions, valleys, pinnacles, and detours, life will seem to have none of its magnificent geography, only a length. It began in mystery, and it will end in mystery, but what a savage and beautiful country lies in between."[27]

Chapter V

Teaching in Community
A Subject-Centered Education

To see a World in a Grain of Sand
And a Heaven in a Wild Flower,
Hold Infinity in the palm of your hand
And Eternity in an hour.

—WILLIAM BLAKE, "AUGURIES OF INNOCENCE"[1]

THE THIRD THING

Our knowledge of the world comes from gathering around great things in a complex and interactive community of truth. But good teachers do more than deliver the news from that community to their students. Good teachers replicate the process of knowing by engaging students in the dynamics of the community of truth.

As I make the case that good teaching is always and essentially communal, I am not abandoning my claim that teaching cannot be reduced to technique. Community, or connectedness, is the principle behind good teaching, but different teachers with different gifts create community in surprisingly diverse ways, using widely divergent methods.

Engaging students in the community of truth does not require that we put the chairs in a circle and have a conversation. A sense of connectedness can also be generated—in classes large and small—through lectures, lab exercises, fieldwork, service learning, electronic media, and many other pedagogies, traditional and experimental. Like teaching itself, creating educational community can never be reduced to technique. It emerges from a principle that can express itself in endless varieties, depending on the identity and integrity of the teacher.

But our conventional pedagogy emerges from a principle that is hardly communal. It centers on a teacher who does little more than deliver conclusions to students. It assumes that the teacher has all the knowledge and the students have little or none, that the teacher must give and the students must take, that the teacher sets all the standards and the students must measure up. Teacher and students gather in the same room at the same time not to experience community but simply to keep the teacher from having to say things more than once.

In reaction to this scenario, a pedagogy based on an antithetical principle has arisen: students and the act of learning are more important than teachers and the act of teaching. The student is regarded as a reservoir of knowledge to be tapped, students are encouraged to teach each other, the standards of accountability emerge from the group itself, and the teacher's role varies from facilitator to co-learner to necessary evil. It may sound like community, but as I will argue in a moment, it can too easily degenerate into something less than the community of truth.

As the debate swings between the teacher-centered model, with its concern for rigor, and the student-centered model, with its concern for active learning, some of us are torn between the poles. We find insights and excesses in both approaches, and neither seems adequate to the task. The problem, of course, is that we are caught in yet another either-or. Whiplashed, with no way to hold the tension, we fail to find a synthesis that might embrace the best of both.

Perhaps there are clues to a synthesis in the image of the community of truth, where the subject "sits in the middle and knows." Perhaps the classroom should be neither teacher-centered nor student-centered but subject-centered. Modeled on the community of truth, this is a classroom in which teacher and students alike are focused on a great thing, a classroom in which the best features of teacher- and student-centered education are merged and transcended by putting not teacher, not student, but subject at the center of our attention.

If we want a community of truth in the classroom, a community that can keep us honest, we must put a *third thing,* a great thing, at the center of the pedagogical circle. When student and teacher are the only active agents, community easily slips into narcissism, where either the teacher reigns supreme or students can do no wrong. A learning community that embodies both rigor and involvement will elude us until we establish a plumb line that measures teacher and students alike—as great things can do.

True community in any context requires a transcendent third thing that holds both me and thee accountable to something beyond ourselves, a fact well known outside of education. In religious life, when a community attaches ultimacy to its ordained leadership or to the mass mind of its members, it will fall into idolatry until it turns to a transcendent center that can judge both parishioners and priests.

olitical life, when a nation lacks a transcendent center that can fear-mongering leaders and fear-filled followers to purposes ger than their fears, its civic life will degenerate, sometimes into scist evil.

The subject-centered classroom is characterized by the fact that he third thing has a presence so real, so vivid, so vocal, that it can hold teacher and students alike accountable for what they say and do. In such a classroom, there are no inert facts. The great thing is so alive that teacher can turn to student or student to teacher, and either can make a claim on the other in the name of that great thing. Here, teacher and students have a power beyond themselves to contend with—the power of a subject that transcends our self-absorption and refuses to be reduced to our claims about it.

I can illustrate this essential idea with a humble, even humiliating, example. I am thinking of an awkward moment that I—and perhaps you—have known, the moment when I make an assertion about the subject, and a student catches me contradicting something I said earlier or something from the text or something the student knows independently of the text or me.

In a teacher-centered classroom, getting caught in a contradiction feels like a failure. Embarrassed, I may resort to footwork fancy enough to impress Muhammad Ali: "Well, it may sound like a contradiction to you, but if you look at the primary sources on that question—which you probably haven't, since they are still in the original Finnish—you will find that . . ."

But in a subject-centered classroom, gathered around a great thing, getting caught in a contradiction can signify success: now I

Teaching in Community

know that the great thing has such a vivid presence among us that any student who pays attention to it can check and correct me. In this moment, the great thing is no longer confined to what I say about it: students have direct, unmediated access to the subject, and they can use their knowledge to challenge my claims. It is a moment not for embarrassment but for celebrating good teaching, teaching that gives the subject—and the students—lives of their own.

In a subject-centered classroom, the teacher's central task is to give the great thing an independent voice—a capacity to speak its truth quite apart from the teacher's voice in terms that students can hear and understand. When the great thing speaks for itself, teachers and students are more likely to come into a genuine learning community, a community that does not collapse into the egos of students or teacher but knows itself accountable to the subject at its core.

Lest the subject-centered classroom sound a bit exotic, consider the kindergarten. Watch a good teacher sitting on the floor with a group of five-year-olds, reading a story about an elephant. Viewed through the eyes of those children, it is almost possible to see that elephant in the middle of the circle! And with that great thing as the vehicle, other great things also come into the room—things like language and the miracle of symbols that carry meaning.

Or consider the service-learning programs that are flourishing on more and more campuses these days, programs that place students in community activities related to the field they are studying. In a large political science class at a state university, three-fourths of the students were assigned a normal syllabus while the remainder were assigned all of that plus a field placement. One might think that the latter students would suffer academically; after all, they had to spend extra time and energy on field assignments and might even have resented that fact. But those students did *better* academically and became more personally and substantively engaged with the course because the great things they met by being involved with the community made their bookwork more real.[2]

Or consider the way students are now learning by means of digital technology—a remarkable way to hold great things at the center of our attention, if my own experience is any measure. I have long been spellbound by the solar system and its workings, but neither the astronomy classes I took in college nor the books I later read satisfied my hunger to understand. But recently, sitting at my computer, using an astronomy "lab" on CD-ROM, I have started to digest the fundamentals of that discipline in a deeply fulfilling way.

One reason for my accelerated learning is the computer's power to create virtual reality. With it, I can make and manipulate models of the planets, their moons, their relationships, and the play of gravity that allow me to place this immensity at the center of my attention, then walk around it and into it as if it were my home (which, in a way I now understand more vividly, it is!). At the same time, I have immediate access to photographs and technical information to refine my understanding, as well as charts that tell me where to look in the night sky. Using similar technology, students in many classrooms are now able to relate more personally to great things in disciplines ranging from architecture to zoology.

It is ironic that objectivism, which *seems* to put the object of knowledge above all else, fosters in practice a teacher-centered classroom. Objectivism is so obsessed with protecting the purity of knowledge that students are forbidden direct access to the object of study, lest their subjectivity defile it. Whatever they know about it must be mediated through the teacher, who stands in for the object, serves as its mouthpiece, and is the sole focus of the student's attention.

At its extreme, this purist approach is represented by the math professor who resisted the movement to reform pedagogy in his discipline with the following claim: "Our primary responsibility as mathematicians is not to students but to mathematics: to preserve, create, and enhance good mathematics and to protect the subject for future generations." Good students, he claimed, the ones destined to become mathematicians, "will survive any educational system, and those are the ones with whom our future lies."[3]

The idea of a student-centered classroom arose from such abuses of the teacher-centered model, but it has encouraged abuses of its own. In a student-centered setting, there is sometimes a tendency toward mindless relativism: "One truth for you, another truth for me, and never mind the difference." When students are put at the center of the circle, teachers may yield too much of their leadership; it is difficult to confront ignorance and bias in individuals or the group when students themselves comprise the plumb line.

Having seen the possibility of a subject-centered classroom, I now listen anew to students' stories about their great teachers in which "a passion for the subject" is a trait so often named (a passion that need not be noisy but can be quietly intense). I always thought that passion made a teacher great because it brought contagious energy into the classroom, but now I realize its deeper function. Passion for the subject propels that subject, not the teacher, into the center of the learning circle—and when a great thing is in their midst, students have direct access to the energy of learning and of life.

A subject-centered classroom is not one in which students are ignored. Such a classroom honors one of the most vital needs our students have: to be introduced to a world larger than their own experiences and egos, a world that expands their personal boundaries and enlarges their sense of community. This is why students often describe great teachers as people who "bring to life" things that the students had never heard of, offering them an encounter with otherness that brings the students to life as well.

A subject-centered classroom also honors one of our most vital needs as teachers: to invigorate those connections between our subjects, our students, and our souls that help make us whole again and again. By putting the "Secret" that Frost wrote about at the center of the circle, we re-member the passion that brought us into this work in the first place—a re-membering that cannot happen when we and our students sit in that circle alone.

TEACHING FROM THE MICROCOSM

When I remind myself that to teach is to create a space in which the community of truth is practiced—that I need to spend less time filling the space with data and my own thoughts and more time opening a space where students can have a conversation with the subject and with each other—I often hear an inner voice of dissent: "But my field is full of factual information that students must possess before they can continue in the field."

This voice urges me to do what I was trained to do: fully occupy the space with my knowledge, even if doing so squeezes my students out. As I listen to this voice, the model of a subject-centered classroom becomes appealing for the wrong reason: I could misuse it as an excuse to fill all the space with the informational demands of the subject itself.

When I succumb to that temptation, it is not merely because of my training or because I have an ego that wants to be at center stage. Like many other teachers I know, I fill the space because I have a professional ethic, one that holds me responsible both for my subject's integrity and for my students' need to be prepared for further education or the job market. To quote many faculty who feel driven by it, it is an ethic that requires us to "cover the field."

This sense of responsibility cannot be faulted. But the conclusion that we draw from it—that we must sacrifice space in order to cover the field—is based on the false premise that *space* and *stuff* are mutually exclusive. To teach in the community of truth, we must find some way to transform this apparent contradiction into a paradox, one that honors both the stuff that must be learned and the space that learning requires.

We can begin with a simple pedagogical fact: if the aim of a course is to deliver a great deal of information, the worst way to do it is by nonstop lecturing (although lecturing can serve other purposes quite well, in ways I will describe later). The human brain is simply not good at retaining armies of facts as they march single-file through a lecture laden with information. Facts are far better delivered via texts or electronic formats, where students can do with them what the brain requires: look at them once, look at them again, and check them once more, then massage them, correlate them, and apply them—in brief but frequent installments.

When facts about the subject are dumped en masse, students are overwhelmed, and their grasp of the facts is fleeting. Knowing this, we might revisit the metaphor of covering the field, which unconsciously portrays teaching as the act of drawing a tarp over a field of grass until no one can see what is under it and the grass dies and nothing new can grow. That is not a bad description of what happens to students in fact-laden courses: they fail to understand the subject, retaining the information just long enough to pass the test, and they never want to pick up a book on that subject again.

How can we reconcile the demands of space and stuff? Some approaches began to emerge for me when I asked myself, "What is the optimum use of the brief time my students and I share in the space called the classroom?"

Rather than use that space to tell my students everything practitioners know about the subject—information they will neither retain nor know how to use—I need to bring them into the circle of practice in that field, into its version of the community of truth. To do so, I can present small but critical samples of the data of the field to help students understand how a practitioner in this field generates data, checks and corrects data, thinks about data, uses and applies data, and shares data with others.

That is, I can teach more with less, simultaneously creating space and honoring the stuff in question. Yet how can a small but critical sample of data adequately represent the vastness of any field, of the great things we are trying to understand? The answer comes as we remember that every discipline has a gestalt, an internal logic, a patterned way of relating to the great things at its core.

Thus every discipline is like a hologram, the model mentioned in Chapter IV that some physicists use to describe the underlying logic of reality itself. A hologram is an ordering of visual data that we regard as remarkable for the way it allows us to see a three-dimensional object on a two-dimensional surface. But a hologram has an even more remarkable trait: every part of the hologram contains all of the information possessed by the whole.

As one physicist describes it, "If the film of a rose hologram is cut in half and then illuminated by a laser, each half will still be found to contain the entire image of the rose. If the halves are divided again, each snippet of film will always be found to contain a smaller but intact version of the original image."[4] Take any piece of a hologram and from it you can reconstruct the whole.

Holographic logic was anticipated two and a half centuries ago by William Blake in a simple image from "Auguries of Innocence," where he suggests that we can "see a World in a Grain of Sand."[5] Every academic discipline has such "grains of sand" through which its world can be seen. So why do we keep dumping truckloads of sand on our students, blinding them to the whole, instead of lifting up a grain so they can learn to see for themselves? Why do we keep trying to cover the field when we can honor the stuff of the discipline more profoundly by teaching less of it at a deeper level?

Each discipline has an inner logic so profound that every critical piece of it contains the information necessary to reconstruct the whole—if it is illuminated by a laser, a highly organized beam of light. That laser is the act of teaching.

This theory may seem difficult to translate into practice, but it is implemented every day in some of our most time-honored pedagogies. Consider the science lab. Here are thirty botany students peering through thirty microscopes at stem sections from the same plant. Alone and together, guided by a teacher, they examine *this* grain of sand, and in the process, they learn the logic of the discipline, its rules of observation and interpretation, as well as some substantive facts. What they discover by examining this microcosm—then another, and another, and another—can eventually translate into literacy in the discipline at large. By diving deep into particularity, these students are developing an understanding of the whole.

No matter what great thing we are studying, there is always an equivalent to the stem section under the microscope. In every great novel, there is a passage that when deeply understood, reveals how the author develops character, establishes tension, creates dramatic movement. With that understanding, the student can read the rest of the novel more insightfully. In every period of history, there is an event that when deeply understood, reveals not only how historians do their work but also illumines the general dynamics of that epoch. In the work of every philosopher, there is a pivotal idea that when deeply understood, reveals the foundations of his or her system or nonsystem of thought.

By teaching this way, we do not abandon the ethic that drives us to cover the field—we honor it more deeply. Teaching from the microcosm, we exercise responsibility toward both the subject and our students by refusing merely to send data "bites" down the intellectual food chain but by helping our students understand where the information comes from and what it means. We honor both the discipline and our students by teaching them how to think like historians or biologists or literary critics rather than merely how to lip-sync the conclusions others have reached.

I want to offer two real-life examples of how teaching from the microcosm can be done in fact-laden fields. In the next section, I tell a large story about the reform of medical education. In the section after that, I tell a small story about my own course in methods of social research. With these stories, I hope to show not only that teaching from the microcosm works in the real world but also that it can work better than our well-meant but misguided attempts to cover the field.

THE MICROCOSM IN MEDICAL SCHOOL

At a large research university where I had spoken about community in education, I was invited to lunch by the dean of the medical school, who said he had a story that might interest me.

Several years earlier, he and a few colleagues had become concerned about the kinds of doctors their students were becoming. The compassion that had led many of these students to enter medical school had largely disappeared by the time they completed their studies. They came into the program caring deeply about people and their health, but four years later, they tended to treat patients as objects to be repaired if possible and overlooked if not.

The dean and his colleagues also worried that too few of their graduates had learned how to learn. They had mastered the aggregation of theory and fact taught in the conventional curriculum, but nothing in that curriculum taught them how to keep current with a fast-flowing stream of knowledge that will look quite different in a few years than it does right now.

So the dean and his small band began advocating an alternative approach. To explain its significance, the dean offered me this image of a traditional medical education:

> For the first two years, the students sit in an auditorium while a professor up on the stage, pointer in hand, goes through the bones of a skeleton hanging from a rack. The students' task is to memorize all that information, feed it back on tests, and use it in laboratory settings.
>
> Then, at the beginning of the third year, they meet their first live patient—and we wonder why they treat that patient like a skeleton hanging from a rack! To say nothing of the fact that this sort of hand-me-down learning gives students no experience at finding things out for themselves.

But objectifying the patient and "dumbing down" the students were not the only problems that worried the dean and his colleagues. They were also concerned about an academic culture that motivated their students to learn not in order to treat patients but to best one another in competition—which led to some sad outcomes.

Occasionally, a professor would place an assigned journal article on reserve in the library, but when the fourth or fifth student went to read it, someone seeking advantage would have cut it out with a razor. Once again, compassion for the patient had disappeared, for the information in that article might have helped a doctor treat a patient some day. Once again, students failed to learn how to learn in a self-motivating manner and learned only to win at the expense of one another.

So the dean and his allies proposed a new approach, originally developed at McMaster University in Hamilton, Ontario. Its key feature is that students, from their first day in medical school, are gathered in small circles around a live patient with a real problem and are asked to diagnose the patient's condition and prescribe a course of treatment.

The dean was quick to assure me that there is a mentor in each circle, a teaching physician who makes sure that this band of amateurs does not do the patient harm. But the mentor's job is not to tell the students what the diagnosis or the prescription is. The mentor is there to guide a collective inquiry into the "great thing"—the patient and the question of illness and health—that has been placed at the center of the students' attention.

The dean explained:

> On one level, the students sitting in that circle do not know very much. Some of them have no premed training at all, since we admit all kinds of majors to medical school these days, and even those with a premed background have no real clinical training.
>
> But on another level, these students know a lot. As individuals, they know something simply because all of them have been sick and have known people who were sick, so they have experiential clues about illness and health.
>
> As a group, they know even more. Here sits a student who has a gift for observation, who is noticing the dullness of the patient's eyes. There sits a student with a gift for intuition, who is picking up information from the patient's body language. And there is a

student with a gift for asking questions, who can get more information from the patient in a few minutes than most of us could get in an hour.

If you can get all of those people and their perceptions to multiply exponentially in a good group process, it is sometimes possible for a collection of amateurs to come up with solid insights.

In this model of medical education, that small circle of students around a patient, that small version of the community of truth, is the hub that turns a larger wheel. From this hub, this living center, students move out to other educational settings for insights not available at the hub—to the library for independent research, to lecture halls for systematic data on various topics, and to seminars, workshops, and labs for practice in the use of particular skills. But wherever they go, they always return to the hub with new facts and theories that help them understand the patient and the problem. Then they go out from the hub again with new questions that focus the knowledge they gather in other venues.

The dean and his allies proposed this model, and after considerable debate within the larger faculty, it was narrowly adopted. When the dust settled, the dissenting faculty made two predictions. The good news was that the new pedagogy would surely improve the bedside manner and medical ethics of their graduates. But the bad news was more than enough to overshadow the good.

The new pedagogy, the dissenters said, would cause standardized test scores to go down: nowhere in this curriculum was anyone systematically covering the field and force-feeding students the facts. For all the humanistic merits of the new plan, its failure to "take objective knowledge seriously" would put both the students and the school in jeopardy, for both of them live and die by test scores.

The dean asked if I would care to guess what had happened in the six years since the plan had been adopted. I thought I probably knew, because we do not usually take someone to lunch to tell about our failures. But I wanted to hear the story in the dean's own words.

The critics were right about the improvements in medical ethics and bedside manner. We have not had an article sliced out of a journal for several years, and we continually get reports from patients about how helpful our students are.

However, they were wrong about the objective tests. Not only did the test scores not decline, but they actually started going up, and during the time we have been teaching this way, they have continued, slowly, to rise. In this approach to medical education, our students not only become more caring but also seem to be getting smarter, faster.

Why is this the case? The reason I want briefly to examine relates to the power of teaching from the microcosm in the community of truth—the microcosm in this case being the great thing called the patient at the center of the learning circle. That patient represents the reason most students want to be doctors—to help people get well. So from day one of their medical education, students are engaged by this pedagogy at the level of their original motivation, and they are kept engaged at that level for the duration of their training.

This is one reason for the heightened ethical behavior these students now display—an ethic that, one hopes, will travel with them into professional life. The dean's report that articles are no longer being slashed out of journals suggests that behavior becomes more ethical when a great thing, rather than one's ego, is at the center of one's attention. Those articles stay in the journals because these students get regular reminders that they are learning in order to help people get well, not to best the competition.

But the consequences of putting a great thing at the center of our attention are not only ethical but intellectual as well: these students are "getting smarter, faster." There are at least two reasons for this, and both of them have to do with the pedagogical power of the community of truth.

First, the human brain works best with information presented not in the form of isolated data bits but in patterns of meaningful connection, in a community of data, as it were. Patterning is what happens when students learn their medical facts through a patient's story, for that story offers both internal and external connections: it connects various facts about the patient with each other in a pattern of correlation and interpretation and explanation, and it connects the student with the patient in a pattern of human meaning.

The dean made this point with a comment that is faithful to what we know about how the human brain works: "Twenty years from now, when one of these students is remembering how the kidney functions, he or she is going to remember that information not as a factoid from a textbook but in the context of Mrs. Smith's story." In other words, the memory will take communal form, the form of reality itself.

Second, this community of truth has pedagogical power because it allows students to do their learning together. Though we persist in believing that competition is the best way to motivate people to learn, these students are far more motivated by the fact that their individual learning enables them to contribute to the communal inquiry—or at least not embarrass themselves by letting the group down. Learning together also offers them a chance to look at reality through the eyes of others, instead of forcing them to process everything through their own limited vision. They can check and correct what they see from various vantage points, thus having a chance to come closer to getting it right.

It is said that all of us together are smarter than any one of us alone, and perhaps that maxim is more than wishful thinking. The story of this medical school encourages me in the belief that a pedagogy based on the community of truth is not a romantic fantasy but can be a practical response to some of our most pressing educational needs.

The Microcosm in Social Research

My second example of teaching from the microcosm is considerably more modest than the reform of medical education, so it may help bring this approach closer to everyday practice.

Methods of Social Research is one of the most mind-numbing courses in the social science curriculum because it is typically taught as an endless flow of information. I taught it that way myself for a few years, until my students fell into a coma and I was forced to seek a more life-giving approach. In the university where I was teaching at the time, Methods was a required course that typically drew a hundred and fifty students, so I needed to find a way to simulate the community of truth in a lecture hall, not a cozy seminar room.

To illustrate the simulation I attempted, I will focus on a two-week passage in midcourse. During this time, I wanted my students to learn certain great things about the way social phenomena are known: how to form concepts, develop indicators, collect data with those indicators, correlate those data into patterns, and interpret what those patterns might mean. Naming these goals clearly as the two weeks got under way helped put some boundaries around a space that would soon contain a creative mess.

To put these subjects at the center of our attention, I drew a simple four-cell statistical table on the board—and left it there for the entire two-week period as the "grain of sand" that would focus our exploration (see Figure 5.1). With this table at the center of our circle of inquiry, I taught by asking question after question about it. As the process unfolded, I tried to wait out the silences until responses came; to engage students in dialogue with each other, not just with me; and when the discussion became terminally tangled, to sort things out with a "lecturette," always followed by a fresh round of questioning and conversation. My hope was to take these students so deep into this microcosm of methodology that they would learn the logic of practice in the field, or at least become intelligent consumers of social research.

I do not have enough pages, nor would you have enough patience, to follow every move my students and I made during that two-week passage. But I can suggest what happened by describing our approach to *concept formation*.

Figure 5.1. *The Relation of Income to Race.*

		Race	
		Black	White
	High	15%	45%
Income			
	Low	85	55
		100%	100%

To bring the abstractness of concept formation to earth, I chose to focus our inquiry on *race,* because it is a so obviously a charged issue in our society—and was especially charged at the university where I was teaching at the time. I believed that exploring race as a concept would create the tension necessary to get and hold my students' attention, and so it did.

I began the first session by observing that the researchers who produced this table not only named race as a factor they wanted to study but also apparently found some way to determine the racial classification of the people they interviewed.

"Tell me," I asked, "how do you determine what race a person is?"

A few students stared at me, astonished by the stupidity of my question, but most of them looked away, for the same reason! I had to work hard inwardly just to hold the space, a space of silence and stupefaction in which I was sorely tempted to forget teaching from the microcosm and revert to lecturing.

But I was able to hold out long enough for one student toward the back of the room to raise her hand, tentatively.

"Yes, please, . . ." I said.

"Well, you *look,*" she said. "You just look!"

When one is teaching this way, and the silence has become an agony, any response is welcome; in my relief, it felt as if this student had just discovered the general theory of relativity! I thanked her for her response and then pressed nervously on.

"Tell me," I asked, "what do you look *for?*"

Now even more students were convinced that I had lost my mind, but the energy level rose a bit, perhaps because they smelled blood.

"Well, you look for color, skin color!" said someone closer to the front, with hints of exasperation and amusement.

"Thank you," I said. "Now let's look at the faces around this room. There seem to be ten or twelve skin colors in here, ranging from a deep ebony to a pale white. Does this mean that we have ten or twelve races in this room, or does it simply mean that some of you white folks have been spending time in the sun?"

On and on the dialogue went, sometimes frustrating, sometimes funny. But step by awkward step, we worked our way toward a fundamental fact about "race."

To the extent that race is even a valid concept—a question that my students took more seriously after our discussion—it does not come in boxes provided by God or Mother Nature. Race is an undifferentiated continuum of gene frequencies that we break into categories through an act called concept formation. We place markers at various points on that genetic continuum: cross this one and you are Caucasian, cross that one and you are African, cross another and you are Asian.

As our inquiry went on, my students began to understand several important things about the demands of concept formation. The concept called race is an artifact of the way our minds divvy up and simplify an intricate body of information about human beings. The shape of that artifact is not an idle matter—for better and for worse, the way we conceptualize race makes a difference in this world.

Because the concept of race makes a difference, socially and scientifically, it is important to know whether there are legitimate rules for divvying up the data. Is concept formation an arbitrary act, guided only by social bias, or are there ways of breaking into that continuum of gene frequencies that are more faithful to the data—and to human beings—than others?

Of course, there are legitimate rules, and my students were more eager to learn them, because through their own engagement with the microcosm and with the issues it posed, they had come into a deeper understanding of the stakes inherent in defining race than any I could have handed them in a lecture.

The understanding they achieved went beyond the particularities of race to the underlying dynamics of any concept. Some of those students may use their knowledge to become creators of new concepts—knowing now, as they do, the norms of discernment that allow one to stake out a pattern of data and lay claim to a new bit of knowledge. Others may become more discerning as both listeners and speakers. They will be unwilling to accept the careless use of other concepts, like *gender* or *nationality,* now that they know how much depends on the way our minds "connect the dots" and frame the phenomena of experience.

Before I taught from the microcosm, I gave decent lectures on these matters, and my students learned significant things. But when I taught from the microcosm, taking less space for my words and opening more space for my students to get involved with the subject, they learned more and they learned it better—learned not only some things that social scientists know but something about doing social science for themselves.

OPEN SPACE AND SKILLFUL MEANS

No matter how many success stories I collect, from other educators or from my own experience, when I try to teach by creating space in which the community of truth can be practiced, I struggle against the strong currents of my own training.

Like most professionals, I was taught to occupy space, not open it: after all, we are the ones who know, so we have an obligation to tell others all about it! Even though I have rejected that nonsensical norm, I still feel guilty when I defy it. A not-so-small voice within me insists that if I am not filling all the available space with my own knowledge, I am not earning my keep.

I know doctors who have a similar struggle when they invite patients to collaborate in their own diagnosis and treatment, instead of simply telling them what is "broken" and how medical science can fix it—or has determined that it cannot be fixed. Virtually all professionals have been deformed by the myth that we serve our clients best by taking up all the space with our hard-earned omniscience.

Our resistance to opening rather than filling the space is compounded by the fact that if we decide to change the way we practice our craft, it takes time to make the transition—and while we are in transit, we are not very good at what we are doing. En route to a new pedagogy, there will be days when we serve our students poorly, days when our guilt only deepens.

To counteract guilt, I need at least two things: a rationale for what I am doing when I open a learning space—which is why I am writing this chapter!—and an understanding of the skillful means required to keep such a space open.

As long as our only test of professional competence is the ability to fill the space—while creating space means merely to go with the flow—we will never be able to open the classroom to the community of truth. As long as we do not understand that opening a learning space requires more skill and more authority than filling it up, we will lose our battle with guilt, and our teaching will default to covering the field. If we want to honor and develop the skills required to create a space for learning, we must name them and make them explicit.

Some of these skills are needed even before the class begins—in conceptualizing the course of study, selecting materials, framing assignments and exercises, and blocking out the time. If I do not make these decisions in ways consonant with opening space, the space will disappear before the class begins.

I must define the course in a way more engaging than engorging, countering my tendency to inundate students with data, and allowing them instead to encounter the subject, each other, and themselves. I must provide readings with substance that students need to know, but with gaps in which students can think their own thoughts—and because this virtue is most often found in primary texts, I must be well acquainted with the literature of my field. I must create exercises that invite students to probe the unknown, as well as exercises that reveal what they have learned. I must establish a schedule that allows time for the unexpected, even as it makes time to acquire the predictably necessary facts.

Preparing a learning space requires at least as much competence as preparing a good lecture—and more than preparing a bad one. But despite the competence required to fulfill this list of "musts," I have not yet walked through the classroom door. When that door closes behind me, another set of skills is required to use and protect the space. For example, in the Methods course, I relied on the skill called questioning—which sounded easy to me until I tried it. Then I discovered the enormous variety of questions I had to choose among.

Some questions close down the space and keep students from thinking: "What did the textbook have to say about concepts and indicators in Chapter Four?" Other questions open up so much space that they lose students in a trackless wasteland: "What is going on in this four-cell table?" The questions that help people learn are found somewhere between these extremes: "If you had been one of these researchers, how would you have decided what race your subjects were?"

Of course, the skill of asking questions goes beyond asking the right kinds of questions to asking them in a manner neither threatening nor demeaning—and receiving responses in the same open and inviting way. Every good teacher knows how easy it is to respond with the right words but dismissive nonverbal judgments—and how quickly this will freeze the discussion.

When we learn to ask good questions, we discover that yet another competence is needed: the ability to turn a question-and-answer session between the teacher and individual students into a complex communal dialogue that bounces all around the room. My students will learn much more when I turn their eyes from always looking at me and help them look at one another.

I must deflect comments addressed to me and bounce them back to the group, perhaps simply by saying, "What do you all think about the point that Sandra just made?" but preferably by being more subtle. However I do it, this deflecting involves a challenge to my soul: I must learn how to trust that the community has the resources necessary to deal with the issue at hand.

I feel that challenge most urgently when a student says something utterly untrue—and everything in me wants to rise up and smite this falsehood with the Sword of Truth. If I want to encourage the conversation that the community of truth requires, I must learn to ask myself in that crucial instant a simple but demanding question: How quickly do I need to do the smiting? Can it wait thirty seconds? A minute? To the end of the hour? Until the next class?

As I consider my options, it becomes clearer that I need not smite immediately. Even with that untruth before us, we—and truth—will survive a few more minutes or hours or days. Then, as I step back from my sense of urgency, it becomes more and more likely that someone else in the group will step forward to challenge what has been said. When that happens, the community of truth comes more fully to life.

But if I learn to ask good questions, deflect answers, and connect my students in dialogue, the job is still not done. I must learn the skill of lifting up and reframing what my students are saying so that we will have benchmarks of how far we have come and how far we have to go toward whatever we are trying to learn.

The richness of the community of truth lies in the fact that its process is nonlinear. Its tracks lead in diverse directions, sometimes circling back on themselves, sometimes jumping far ahead. In the midst of this creative chaos, the teacher must know when and how to draw a straight line by connecting comments that have been made, revealing a trajectory of inquiry that can both confirm what we know and take us somewhere new.

To do this, I must listen so attentively to what my students say that I can relate the comment just now made to one made twenty minutes ago. Attentive listening is never an easy task—it consumes psychic energy at a rate that tires and surprises me. But it is made easier when I am holding back my own authoritative impulses. When I suspend, for just a while, my inner chatter about what I am going to say next, I open room within myself to receive the external conversation.

Once I have listened and traced a trajectory, I am ready to reframe—to articulate what we have learned in a way that relates it to where we have been and where we are about to go. For example, my students in the Methods course came close, on their own, to the insight that race is a mental construct rather than a biological reality. Yet they never quite made the leap into framing it as an "undifferentiated continuum of gene frequencies that we break into categories."

My students lacked that language, so it was my task to reframe the scattered pieces of our conversation. But I needed to wait for the moment when my students could experience it as their own, as a way of naming a discovery that they had made for themselves but were not yet able to put into words. With that reframing, we accomplished three important things: we gathered up the elements of our dialogue and gave them coherence, we built a bridge to our next topic, and we did it all in a way that made students full participants in this miniature version of the community of truth.

By reconstructing the dynamics of teaching and learning in the community of truth, I remind myself that teaching this way involves much more than going with the flow. I must hone certain skills and learn others as I go to make a space for this kind of education to happen.

COMMUNITY: VARIETIES AND OBSTACLES

Engaging students in the dynamics of the community of truth is a principle of sound pedagogy. But the methods I have examined for creating that community in the classroom are neither normative nor exhaustive. The "right" method to use in replicating the community of truth is one that emerges from the identity and integrity of the teacher.

What seems right for me, after many years of searching, is to sit in a circle with my students (or try to relate to the crowd in a lecture hall as if we were in a circle) and lead an inquiry into the great thing in our midst. But there are other ways to create community in the classroom, and some of them look nothing like the interactive encounter we normally associate with that word.

I need only recall the mentor I wrote about in Chapter I. In his courses on the history of social thought, he lectured nonstop while we sat in rows and took notes. But those classes were not teacher-centered: his lectures put the subject, not himself, at the center of our attention, and we somehow gathered around that subject and interacted with it, though we said hardly a word.

How did my mentor manage to simulate the community of truth and draw his students into it? His lectures did not merely present the data of social theory; they staged the drama of social thought. He did this in part by telling stories from the lives of great thinkers as well as explaining their ideas. We could almost see Karl Marx, sitting alone in the British Museum Library writing *Das Kapital*. Through active imagination we were brought into relationship with the thinker himself and with the personal and social conditions that stimulated his thought.

But the drama of my mentor's lectures went further still. He would make a strong Marxist statement, and we would transcribe it in our notebooks as if it were holy writ. Then a puzzled look would pass over his face. He would pause, step to one side, turn and look back at the space he had just exited, and argue with his own statement from an Hegelian point of view! This was not an artificial device but a genuine expression of the intellectual drama that continually occupied this teacher's mind and heart.

Drama does not mean histrionics, of course, and remembering that fact can help us name a form of community that is palpable and powerful without being overtly interactive or even face to face. When I see a good play, I sometimes feel strongly connected to the drama, as if my own life were being portrayed on the stage. But I have no desire to respond aloud to the line just spoken, no urge to run up the aisle, jump onto the stage, and join in the action. Sitting in the audience, I am already on stage "in person," connected in an inward and invisible way that we rarely credit as the powerful form of community that it is.

With a good drama, I do not need overt interaction to be "in community" with the characters and their lives. Similarly, when a good lecture places the drama of great things squarely in our midst, it can manifest the community of truth as fully, in its own way, as that medical school curriculum or my dialogical approach to Methods of Social Research.

I used to wonder how my mentor, who was so awkward in his face-to-face relations with students, managed to simulate the community of truth so well. Now I understand: he was continually in community without us! Who needs twenty-year-olds from the suburbs when you are hanging out with the likes of Marx, Hegel, Durkheim, Weber, and Troeltsch?

Yet this man, though he communed more intimately with the great figures of social thought than with the people close at hand, cared deeply about his students. The passion with which he lectured was not only for his subject but also for us to know his subject. He wanted us to meet and learn from the constant companions of his intellect and imagination, and he made those introductions in a way that was deeply integral to his own nature.

Through this teacher and his lectures, some of us joined a powerful form of community marked by the ability to talk with the dead. This is not a mark of madness but of an educated person. Learning to speak and listen in that invisible community of history and thought makes one's world immeasurably larger and forever changes one's life.

But to some teachers who care about these things, it makes no difference whether we define community as overt interaction or as drama or as inward dialogue. These teachers claim that education will never achieve community in any form as long as teacher-student relations are riddled with inequalities in status and power. Teachers must evaluate and grade the work students do—which sets teachers against students and students against each other. How is community possible when such divisive dynamics are at work?

The question assumes that community can happen only where there are no divisions of status and power—but such places do not exist. If community is to emerge, it will have to be in the midst of inequalities that appear whenever two or three are gathered. To argue that grades must be eliminated before community can emerge is to assume a utopian alternative nowhere to be found: it is to give up on community altogether.

When authentic community emerges, false differences in power and status disappear, such as those based on gender or race. But real differences remain, and so they should, for they are created by functions that need to be performed if community is to thrive—such as the leadership task of maintaining the boundaries and upholding the standards that define community at its best.

Evaluation is one such function in education. The community of truth demands continual discernment: some observations are accurate and some are not; some claims of fact are valid and others are not; some hypotheses are warranted and others are not. When grades are used to make distinctions of this sort, they are simply a replication of the real-world dynamics that this approach to teaching is built on.

With this real-world principle in mind, we can invent ways of using grades that emphasize learning rather than judging and collaboration rather than competition, thus enhancing the contributions grades can make to community. For example, I offer students the chance to rewrite a term paper as often as they like before the course ends. I grade each version, commenting on its strengths and weaknesses. When I give a final grade, it is not an average but the grade given for the last version. In this way, I hope to show students that the intent of evaluation is to offer guidelines for learning rather than terminal judgments.

I also give assignments that require students to work together on a project—with the understanding that they will all receive the same grade for the final product, not different grades for the different parts they contributed. Grading represents power, and the question we should ask is not how to get rid of our power but how to use it toward better ends.

I am not suggesting that letter grades are a good form of evaluation; they are a very poor form indeed compared to more nuanced methods like the student portfolio. But grades have been with us for a long time and will be for years to come, so it would be wrong to use them as a cheap excuse for avoiding the challenges of community in the classroom.

The real threat to community in the classroom is not power and status differences between teachers and students but the lack of interdependence that those differences encourage. Students are dependent on teachers for grades—but what are teachers dependent on students for? If we cannot answer that question with something as real to us as grades are to students, community will not happen. When we are not dependent on each other, community cannot exist.

The problem is that we who teach have been trained, like most professionals, to work in utter autonomy, a mode that makes us and our destinies largely independent of our students. To put it baldly, we do not need them to succeed.

Our superior power and status *permit* us to work this way, but they do not *compel* us to work this way. It is possible to teach in a manner that puts part of our fate into the hands of students, as part of their fate is in ours. Such a way of teaching yields not only more community but also more learning by drawing us more deeply into the community of truth.

I can illustrate with a story about a guest lecture I was once invited to give. The professor said that the session ran an hour and a half, and when I responded that I would lecture for only twenty to thirty minutes, then open things up for discussion, she urged me not to do so. "This is a big class," she said, "about one hundred fifty students, and they are accustomed to lectures, not discussion. I'm afraid your approach won't work very well."

I persisted in my plans, but when the day arrived and I was about halfway into my talk before a sea of impassive faces, I began to think that my host had been right. When I finished talking and asked who wanted to get us started with a comment or a question—nervously violating my own rule of asking questions that are specific and concrete!—I wished that I had taken her advice: this felt less and less like a guest appearance and more and more like a public hanging.

Then, as sometimes happens, a student who seemed as anxious as I, perhaps because she felt sorry for me, raised her hand and asked a question, and I responded. That exchange led to a couple of other hands' being raised and on to more and more exchanges. The energy rose, and after a while, a real conversation emerged, multiple in its levels but steady in its direction.

When it was time to leave, I thanked the students in the class for a fine session. They applauded enthusiastically, and about twenty of them came up front to talk. After ten minutes, the next class started arriving, so we adjourned to the hallway, where a dozen of us continued talking for another ten or fifteen minutes. It was clear that some real learning had happened for a good number of people.

As my host walked me to the parking lot, she said, "That was remarkable! I've never seen this class so animated. I noticed that you used a couple of clever techniques to stimulate conversation." She obviously did not know me very well, or she would not have accused me of "technique"!

But I was curious: "What do you mean?"

She said, "Every time a hand went up, no matter how tentatively, you leaned forward, motioned toward the person like this," she made a "c'mon" gesture with her hand, "and you said, 'Please . . .' Then, no matter what that person said, you smiled and said, 'Thank you,' like you really meant it."

My host seemed to feel that these were strategic moves designed to manipulate the group's emotions, but that is not the case. They were the desperate actions of a dying man!

There is a name for those moments when I said "please" and gestured imploringly—it is called begging. There is a name for those moments when I said "thank you" for the smallest crumb—it is called gratitude. When you are starving, you beg for help without shame, and you are genuinely grateful for anything anyone offers. I had run out of lecture that morning with an hour left to go, and I needed the help of those students if our encounter was to be worthwhile.

When we are willing to abandon our self-protective professional autonomy and make ourselves as dependent on our students as they are on us, we move closer to the interdependence that the community of truth requires. When we can say "please" because we need our students and "thank you" because we are genuinely grateful for them, obstacles to community will begin to fall away, teachers and students will meet at new depths of mutuality and meaning, and learning will happen for everyone in surprising and life-giving ways.

Chapter VI

Learning in Community
The Conversation of Colleagues

"The best thing for being sad," replied Merlyn . . . "is to learn something. That is the only thing that never fails. You may grow old and trembling in your anatomies, you may lie awake at night listening to the disorder of your veins, . . . you may see the world around you devastated by evil lunatics, or know your honor trampled in the sewers of baser minds. There is only one thing for it then—to learn. Learn why the world wags and what wags it. That is the only thing which the mind can never exhaust, never alienate, never be tortured by, never fear or distrust, and never dream of regretting. Learning is the thing for you."

— T. H. WHITE, *The Once and Future King*[1]

TEACHING BEHIND CLOSED DOORS

When I imagine the community of truth gathered around some great thing—from DNA to *The Heart of Darkness* to the French Revolution— I wonder: Could teachers gather around the great thing called "teaching and learning" and explore its mysteries with the same respect we accord any subject worth knowing?

We need to learn how to do so, for such a gathering is one of the few means we have to become better teachers. There are no formulas for good teaching, and the advice of experts has but marginal utility. If we want to grow in our practice, we have two primary places to go: to the inner ground from which good teaching comes and to the community of fellow teachers from whom we can learn more about ourselves and our craft.

If I want to teach well, it is essential that I explore my inner terrain. But I can get lost in there, practicing self-delusion and running in self-serving circles. So I need the guidance that a community of collegial discourse provides—to say nothing of the support such a community can offer to sustain me in the trials of teaching and the cumulative and collective wisdom about this craft that can be found in every faculty worth its salt.

Resources that could help us teach better are available from each other—if we could get access to them. But there, of course, is the rub. Academic culture builds barriers between colleagues even higher and wider than those between us and our students. These barriers come partly from the competition that keeps us fragmented by fear. But they also come from the fact that teaching is perhaps the most privatized of all the public professions.

Though we teach in front of students, we almost always teach solo, out of collegial sight—as contrasted with surgeons or trial lawyers, who work in the presence of others who know their craft well. Lawyers argue cases in front of other lawyers, where gaps in their skill and knowledge are clear for all to see. Surgeons operate under the gaze of specialists who notice if a hand trembles, making malpractice less likely. But teachers can lose sponges or amputate the wrong limb with no witnesses except the victims.

When we walk into our workplace, the classroom, we close the door on our colleagues. When we emerge, we rarely talk about what happened or what needs to happen next, for we have no shared experience to talk about. Then, instead of calling this the isolationism it is and trying to overcome it, we claim it as a virtue called "academic freedom": my classroom is my castle, and the sovereigns of other fiefdoms are not welcome here.

We pay a high price for this privatization. Consider the way teaching is evaluated. When we cannot observe each other's teaching, we get evaluation practices that are distanced, demoralizing, and even disreputable. Lacking firsthand information about each other's work, we allow the artifacts of the student survey to replace the facts that can be known only in person.

The normal mode of "evaluating" teaching is to give students, toward the end of a course, a standardized questionnaire that reduces this complex craft to ten or fifteen dimensions, measured on a five-point scale: "Gives clear and concise instructions"; "Organizes lectures well"; "Establishes objective criteria for grading."

Teachers have every right to be demoralized by such a simplistic approach—the nuances of teaching cannot possibly be captured this way. No uniform set of questions will apply with equal force to the many varieties in which good teaching comes. But if we insist on closing the door on our work, how can others evaluate us except by tossing some questionnaires over the transom just before the end of the term? Evaluations of this sort are not simply the result of administrative malfeasance, as faculty sometimes complain. They are the outcome of a faculty culture that offers no alternative.

Sadly, the limitations of these evaluations are so cynically accepted, and their outcomes so selectively invoked, that the data are easily used in an institutional shell game. If we want to fire someone who has good teaching evaluations but few publications, we argue that the questionnaire merely measures popularity. If we want to promote someone who has poor teaching evaluations but many publications, we argue that the questionnaire has no relevance to the rigorous scholarship he or she imparts.

There is only one honest way to evaluate the many varieties of good teaching with the subtlety required: it is called being there. We must observe each other teach, at least occasionally—and we must spend more time talking to each other about teaching. Then, when the time comes for promotion and tenure decisions, we will have real information to work with, rather than the statistical fictions with which we now manipulate decisions.

I realize that busy schedules prevent teachers from being in each other's classes very often. But if we had periodic conversations with each other about teaching over an extended period of time, we would know enough about each other to ask real questions and give real answers when the moment for evaluation arrived:

- Does this person take teaching seriously, as signified by his or her involvement in conversations about it?
- What kind of process does this person go through in designing a course?
- How does this person identify and respond to the problems that arise as a course proceeds?

- Does this person learn from past mistakes in designing and implementing future courses?
- Does this person attempt to help colleagues with issues in their teaching?

Involvement in a community of pedagogical discourse is more than a voluntary option for individuals who seek support and opportunities for growth. It is a professional obligation that educational institutions should expect of those who teach—for the privatization of teaching not only keeps individuals from growing in their craft but fosters institutional incompetence as well. By privatizing teaching, we make it hard for educational institutions to become more adept at fulfilling their mission.

The growth of any craft depends on shared practice and honest dialogue among the people who do it. We grow by private trial and error, to be sure—but our willingness to try, and fail, as individuals is severely limited when we are not supported by a community that encourages such risks. When any function is privatized, the most likely outcome is that people will perform it conservatively, refusing to stray far from the silent consensus on what "works"—even when it clearly does not.

This risk-averse conservatism describes the state of teaching all too well. Compared to other professions, teaching has evolved very slowly because of its privatization. If surgery and the law were practiced as privately as teaching, we would still treat most patients with leeches and dunk defendants in millponds.

The resources we need in order to grow as teachers are abundant within the community of colleagues. How can we emerge from our privatization and create a continuing conversation about pedagogy that will allow us to tap that abundance? Good talk about good teaching is what we need—to enhance both our professional practice and the selfhood from which it comes.

I want to explore three elements essential to encouraging this kind of conversation among colleagues: *topics* that take us beyond technique and into the fundamental issues of teaching, *ground rules* that keep us from defeating ourselves before the talk can go very deep, and *leaders* who expect and invite us to join the conversation.

NEW TOPICS OF CONVERSATION

Our tendency to reduce teaching to questions of technique is one reason we lack a collegial conversation of much duration or depth. Though technique-talk promises the "practical" solutions that we think we want and need, the conversation is stunted when technique is the only topic: the human issues in teaching get ignored, so the human beings who teach feel ignored as well. When teaching is reduced to technique, we shrink teachers as well as their craft—and people do not willingly return to a conversation that diminishes them.

If we do not talk only about methods, what will we talk about? Our options are many and diverse, and we have already explored some of them here. We can talk about the mentors and subjects that evoked the teacher in us, as in Chapter I. We can talk about the human condition of teachers and learners, as in our exploration of fear in Chapter II. Using the concept of paradox, we can talk about classroom highs and lows, our own gifts and limits, and the creation of learning spaces, as in Chapter III. We can talk about ways of knowing and how they shape our ways of teaching, as in Chapters IV and V.

In this chapter, I want to explore two more topics that can generate good talk about good teaching and about the identity from which good teaching comes: critical moments in teaching and learning, and metaphors and images that can enrich our sense of the self who teaches.

"Critical moments" is a simple approach I use in faculty workshops to invite people to share their practice in an open and honest way. I begin by drawing a horizontal arrow on a chalkboard, representing the movement of a course from beginning to end. Then I ask people to name the critical moments they experience along that time line as a course proceeds. By critical moment, I mean one in which a learning opportunity for students will open up, or shut down— depending, in part, on how the teacher handles it. "In part" is an important qualification, for one of the challenges of teaching is the fact that not all critical moments are under the teacher's control.

The moments people name are many and varied. As they are called out, I place each one on the time line at the point, or points, where it tends to happen as a course proceeds, labeling it with a word or two. The line is soon dotted with episodes familiar to every teacher: the first class and the way it sets a tone for the rest of the semester; the first "stupid" question that is asked; the first graded exercise that reveals how few of your students understand the subject; the first challenge to your competence or authority; the first argument that breaks out between students; the first sexist or racist remark.

Not all critical moments involve tension or dissension. Some are more uplifting: when your students understand a topic so well that you need to introduce a new one ahead of schedule; when your students talk so easily with each other that you have a hard time getting a word in edgewise; when something unexpected but important happens in class and your agenda must be scrapped. Each of these moments is full of educational potential—but each can be squandered by a teacher who takes a misstep.

As the critical moments brainstorming continues, a simple but vital thing happens: faculty talk openly about events that have perplexed and defeated them, as well as those they have managed with ease. That is, they do what we must do if we are to help each other grow as teachers: speak openly and honestly about our struggles as well as our successes.

If I asked people flat out to name their classroom dilemmas, we would not reach this level of candor so quickly, if ever. But the open, nondirective nature of this exercise invites honesty because it allows us to identify both highs and lows in a voluntary, descriptive, and nonjudgmental way.

In leading this exercise, I try to make it clear that people are to speak about their own classroom experience and not counsel colleagues on what should happen in *their* classrooms. And on the rare occasion when someone tries to hand out such advice, I ask the person to stop. In the critical moments dialogue, we have a chance to tell it like it is for ourselves, and a sense of community grows as we discover how much we have in common. I am especially touched when young teachers, who believe that their struggles are unique, find relief in the revelation that older faculty still struggle with problems like their own.

As the time line grows, it stops looking like an arrow and starts looking more like a map. Some lines loop around, connecting one classroom moment to another, while other lines trace out-of-class

THE COURAGE TO TEACH

dynamics that bear on the classroom itself (tensions in the dorm, a tragedy on campus, an impending big game). With this complex map before us, we understand something that makes our work more daunting but more intriguing: though teaching sometimes feels like a linear flow of experience from one session to the next, it is actually an intricate patterning of life, with rhythms, textures, and shapes we must attend to, a kind of creative chaos we can learn to enjoy.

The question of how to attend to that complexity leads to the next step in the exercise. Studying the time line and the data of our own experience, we cluster kindred moments together: here is a cluster relating to conflict in the classroom; here is one dealing with the teacher's authority; here is another involving the link between theory and practice.

I ask people to choose a cluster that interests them and form a small group around it, offering each member an opportunity to talk about what he or she has done, for better or for worse, in response to the critical moments in question. Our purpose in the small groups is not to critique each other's pedagogy but to speak honestly from our own experience and listen openly while others do the same. As we do, we are exploring technique—but in a nonreductionistic manner. We are learning about a variety of teaching methods without one or another being promoted as *the* way.

But the inquiry that goes on in these small groups takes us deeper than methodology. As we listen to each other's stories, we are often reflecting silently on our own identity and integrity as teachers. When person A speaks, I realize that the method that works for him would not work for me, for it is not grounded in who I am. But as I listen to person B, I realize that the method she uses is one I would like to learn, for it feels integral to my nature. We have created a conversation that works like a navigator's triangulation, allowing us to locate ourselves more precisely on teaching's inner terrain by noting the position of others—without anyone's being told that he or she should move to a new location.

I want to propose one more topic for good talk about good teaching, one that takes us more directly into the mystery of the teacher's selfhood: generating and exploring metaphors and images of who we are when we are teaching at our best.

In faculty workshops, depending on the readiness of the group, I sometimes ask people to fill in the blank: "When I am teaching at my best, I am like a _____ ." I ask people to do this quickly, accepting the image that arises within them, resisting the temptation to censor or edit it.

The point of the exercise is to allow one's unconscious to surface a metaphor, no matter how silly or strange, that contains an insight that the rational mind would never allow. Not all groups have enough access to their imagination or are sufficiently at home with themselves to take this kind of risk. But when people are willing to feel a bit foolish among colleagues, the payoff in self-understanding can be considerable.

I can illustrate both the risk and the payoff by exploring my own metaphor. It came to me twenty-plus years ago, under conditions long forgotten: when I am teaching at my best, I am like a sheepdog—not the large, shaggy, lovable kind, but the all-business Border collies one sees working the flocks in sheep country.

I once saw such dogs at work in Scotland's rocky fields, and that may be where the image took root in me, though teaching was far from my mind at the time. But as I unfolded the meaning of my metaphor—which I ask teachers in workshops to do with their own—I began to understand how the image of the sheepdog offers some clues to my identity and integrity as a teacher.

In my imagination—unfettered by expert knowledge of the real thing—the sheepdog has four vital functions. It maintains a space where the sheep can graze and feed themselves; it holds the sheep together in that space, constantly bringing back strays; it protects the boundaries of the space to keep dangerous predators out; and when the grazing ground is depleted, it moves with the sheep to another space where they can get the food they need.

It is obvious, I suppose, where I am going with all this, though when I began exploring the image it was not obvious to me. From the crude and uncomfortable metaphor of myself as a sheepdog, I evolved a more refined image of teaching that I have been exploring for several chapters now: to teach is to create a space in which the community of truth is practiced.

My task in the classroom, I came to see, parallels this imaginative rendering of the sheepdog's task. My students must feed themselves—

that is called active learning. If they are to do so, I must take them to a place where food is available: a good text, a well-planned exercise, a generative question, a disciplined conversation. Then, when they have learned what there is to learn in that place, I must move them to the next feeding ground. I must hold the group within those places, paying special attention to individuals who get lost or run away—and all the while I must protect the group from deadly predators, like fear.

Is this the way others should teach? I have no idea. The metaphor behind this approach comes from my unconscious mind, so it reflects, in a naive and primitive way, something of my own identity and integrity. In workshops I have led, people have come up with many fruitful metaphors for themselves, none of which work for me—people for whom teaching at their best is like being a waterfall or a mountain guide or a gardener or a weather system. Good teaching cannot be reduced to technique: good teaching comes from the identity and integrity of the teacher.

We can explore that identity and integrity a bit further by taking two more steps with the metaphor. First, we can look at the shadow it may suggest in us as well as the strengths it reveals. As we have seen before, identity and integrity are not always bright and shining things.

The shadow suggested by my metaphor seems obvious: I have a tendency to regard my students as "sheep" in the invidious way that word can imply. I sometimes get angry about my students' apparent docility or mindlessness or the way they hang their heads down. If I allow this shadow to fall between my students and me, I cannot possibly teach well. If the sheepdog metaphor does nothing else but keep me alert to the appearance of my own shadow, it will have served me, and my students, well.

Second, we can take our metaphor and with the help of others, discover the guidance it may offer for the hard times in our teaching. Consider the second case study I offered in Chapter III, involving my disastrous classroom run-in with the Gang of Three. I can ask myself (with a face as straight as I can muster), "What would a sheepdog have done under those circumstances?"—and then try to answer that question in ways that stay as close to the metaphor as possible, avoiding the literalism of problem solving and technique.

Learning in Community

This exercise, rooted in an image that arises from somewhere in my psyche, saves me from the quick technical fix I always want when I examine a bad moment in teaching. It returns me in imagination to the inner landscape of identity and integrity where my deepest guidance is to be found.

In my case, the guidance seems quite specific. Instead of letting that class unravel, as I did, a sheepdog would have barked and nipped at the wayward sheep early and often enough to keep them from becoming such a well-established distraction. Had they persisted, after repeated warnings, to wander out of reach, the sheepdog would probably have allowed them to face their fate with the wolves rather than sacrificing the rest of the flock, as I did.

A sheepdog would have practiced some form of "tough love" instead of playing the "nice guy" role until things got out of hand. I can translate these metaphorical meanings into all kinds of practical actions, from confronting students more directly about their behavior to using grades *in extremis* for behavioral modification. But the guidance I need, and the power I need to follow it, is in the psychic energy of the metaphor itself.

GROUND RULES FOR DIALOGUE

New topics of conversation can help create good talk about good teaching, but they are not enough. These topics, unlike the more distanced talk about technique, tend to make us vulnerable, so they need to be accompanied by new ground rules for dialogue—rules that will help us respect each other's vulnerability and avoid chilling the conversation before it can even begin.

Without new ground rules, we will revert to the norms implicit in any culture that tell us how we are supposed to talk to each other. In our culture, these include politeness, a ban on inquiring into things that are "none of your business," and a willingness to give the other the benefit of the doubt. In academic settings, these conventional rules are overlaid with another set that encourage competition: we should question each other's claims, think oppositionally about what we are hearing, and be ready with a quick response.

That mix is obviously a recipe for confusion. The conventional norm of "making nice" with each other, folded into the professional norm of competition, creates an ethos in which it feels dangerous to speak or to listen. Then we proceed to multiply that confusion, and the sense of danger that goes with it, by interleaving a third set of norms implicit in conventional and academic culture alike: we were put on earth to advise, fix, and save each other, and whenever an opportunity to do so presents itself, we should seize it!

This fix-it response kicks in almost reflexively when someone breaks free of the first and second set of norms and actually manages to name a real problem he or she is having, for example, in teaching. At the very moment of feeling most vulnerable—having violated norms that tell us to be both guarded and competitive—the person is suddenly invaded with advice: "I used to have that problem, but here is how I solved it," or "You ought to read so-and-so's book. It tells you exactly how to deal with a situation like that."

Sometimes the advice is offered in order to be helpful, and sometimes it is given to make the adviser feel superior. But the motivation does not matter, for the outcome is almost always the same: quick fixes make the person who shared the problem feel unheard and dismissed.

If we want to support each other's inner lives, we must remember a simple truth: the human soul does not want to be fixed, it wants simply to be seen and heard. If we want to see and hear a person's soul, there is another truth we must remember: the soul is like a wild animal—tough, resilient, and yet shy. When we go crashing through the woods shouting for it to come out so we can help it, the soul will stay in hiding. But if we are willing to sit quietly and wait for a while, the soul may show itself.

We need ground rules for dialogue that allow us to be present to another person's problems in a quiet, receptive way that encourages the soul to come forth, a way that does not presume to know what is right for the other but allows the other's soul to find its own answers at its own level and pace.

I have had some experience with a model for this way of being together. It comes from a branch of the Quaker community that for more than three centuries has done without benefit of clerical leadership. In order to do work that most churches do via ordained leaders—like helping people deal with the issues in their lives—these Quakers had to invent social structures that would allow their members to do such work with and for each other.

The ground rules for every social structure they invented had to honor a powerful and paradoxical pair of Quaker beliefs: each of us has an inner teacher that is an arbiter of truth, *and* each of us needs the give-and-take of community in order to hear that inner teacher speak. So Quaker social structures offer community to help a person discover the guidance that comes from within *and* ground rules to prevent that community from invading the individual's inwardness with external agendas and advice.

The Quaker structure I have adapted for use with faculty is called the "clearness committee." It sounds like a name from the '60s, and it is—the 1660s. It is a time-honored process that invites people to help each other with personal problems while practicing a discipline that protects the sanctity of the soul.

Suppose I am wrestling with an issue related to my teaching— from designing a course to be taught next semester to struggling with my anger about students who act up in class. (The former is the kind of problem that most teachers can explore together, because it requires only mild trust; the latter is the kind of issue that will be risked only by people who have real confidence in each other.)

With my problem in mind, I—the so-called focus person in this process—invite four or five colleagues to become members of my clearness committee. Before we meet, I write a few pages about the problem for my colleagues to read. My write-up can take any form, but it often helps to organize it under three headings: first, a clear statement of the nature of the problem itself; second, notes on its relevant background, such as prior situations in which I had a similar experience; and third, notes on its relevant foreground, on what I see on the horizon when I hold this problem in view—for example, that I find the problem so discouraging that I have thought about quitting my job.

People often report that the first step toward clearness comes with putting the problem on paper. Doing so forces us to winnow our feelings and facts, allowing the chaff to blow away and getting the issue outside of our heads, into the light of day, where problems often look different than when we recycle them endlessly through our fears and doubts.

Then the committee meets for two to three uninterrupted hours. Seated in a circle with the focus person, committee members practice the discipline of giving undivided attention to that person

THE COURAGE TO TEACH

and his or her question. For two or three hours, the focus person becomes the great thing at the heart of this small version of the community of truth, the sacred subject, worthy of respect.

Undivided attention means letting the focus person, and his or her issue, be at the center of the circle without trying, as a committee member, to put yourself there. This means that committee members do not call attention to themselves by laughing uproariously when something funny happens or by rushing to comfort the focus person when he or she is feeling pain or by falsely uniting with his or her concern ("I know exactly how you feel"). Undivided attention means forgetting about yourself, and for just a couple of hours, acting as if you had no other purpose on earth than to care for this human being.

The meeting begins with the focus person briefly restating the issue. Then members of the committee begin their work, guided and constrained by the basic and nonnegotiable ground rule of this proceeding: *members are forbidden to speak to the focus person in any way except to ask that person an honest, open question.* The pace of the questioning must be slow—this is a discernment process, not a thesis defense or cross-examination. The focus person usually answers each question aloud but always has the right to pass, leading to the next question and response and the next and the next. By allowing ample silence between a response and the next question, the group keeps the process respectful and gentle.

The ground rule of questions only is simple, but its implications are demanding. It means no advice, no overidentification ("I had that problem once, and here is what I did"), no handing off the problem to someone else ("You ought to talk with X about this"), no suggestions of books to read, techniques to use, meditations to practice, therapists to see. Members of the committee may only ask the focus person honest, open questions—questions that do not promote the questioner's agenda but help the focus person discover wisdom within.

Before a clearness committee convenes, we must remind each other what an honest, open question is, so skilled are we at posing questions that are really advice in disguise. If I ask, "Have you thought about seeing a therapist?" honesty probably requires me to tell you that in my opinion, you should see a therapist. My question cannot be honest and open if, even as I ask it, I am listening for a particular answer that I regard as "correct." But if I ask, "Has this kind of thing ever happened to you before?" and if it has, "How did it make you feel?" my questions are probably open and honest. With questions of this sort, it is unlikely that I hope to hear any particular answer or believe that I know what the "right" answer is.

Over a two-hour period, this cycle of question and response can have remarkable cumulative effect. As the focus person speaks his or her truth, the layers of interference between that person and the inner teacher are slowly stripped away, allowing the person to hear more clearly the guidance that comes from within.

As the process unfolds, we are reminded of a simple truth: because we cannot get inside another person's soul, we cannot possibly know the answer to another person's problem. Indeed, we cannot even know exactly what the problem is. I am often reminded of this fact when I serve as a member of a clearness committee. Ten minutes into the proceedings, I feel certain that I know what is wrong with the focus person and how to fix it. But after two hours of attentive listening, I am appalled at my earlier arrogance. I see now that I did not understand—and even if I did, my abstract concept of the problem is meaningless until understanding arises within the person whose problem it is.

As a member of many clearness committees, I have been privileged to witness a remarkable thing: human beings in dialogue with their inner teachers. Watching the focus person in this setting provides the most vivid evidence I have ever seen that each of us has a teacher within—all we need are the conditions that allow us to listen, to speak, and to learn.

What members of a clearness committee learn about themselves goes unspoken but is important. As we practice the discipline of only asking questions, we open an inner space to receive another person— a space that closes down when we are worrying about how to fix someone or preparing the next comment we want to make. Members often report that the receptive openness they develop in a committee carries over into their relationships with spouses, children, friends, and students.

Yet in that space we receive ourselves as well as the other. As we reach for questions that will help the focus person go deeper into his or her truth, we find ourselves drawn more deeply into our own truth. By the time the process is over, we who have attended faithfully to another person have remembered vital dimensions of our own lives.

Fifteen minutes before the committee is scheduled to end, someone asks the focus person if he or she wants to continue with the questions-only rule or would be willing to accept some mirroring in addition to more questions.

Mirroring does not mean an opportunity to give advice. It means reflecting to the focus person things he or she said or did but might not be aware of: "When asked about A, you said B," or "When you spoke about X, your voice dropped and you seemed tired, but when you spoke about Y, your energy rose and your eyes got bright."

We humans have a curious conceit that just because we have said something, we understand it. But that is not always the case. We may not have heard ourselves say it, and even if we did, we may not yet know what it means. Mirroring gives us a chance to retrieve verbal and nonverbal clues to the resolution of our own dilemmas from a text of our own making.

As the clearness committee comes to an end, two reminders are in order. First, the value of the process is not to be judged by whether the focus person's problem has been "solved." Real life does not work that way. This process is about planting seeds—as in authentic education—and there is no way of knowing when, where, or how those seeds will flower.

Second, everything that went on in the process is guarded by two rules of confidentiality. The first is the conventional rule that whatever was said in the group must remain within it. The second is an uncommon rule of deep confidentiality: When the clearness committee is over, members may not approach the focus person with comments or suggestions, for to do so would violate the spirit of the process. When these rules are understood from the outset, the focus person feels safer about speaking truth—and the rest of us are reminded to honor the solitude of that person's soul long after the committee ends.

Whenever I use the clearness committee in a faculty workshop, even with problems as ordinary as designing a new course, many participants say that they were able to listen to colleagues, and even to themselves, at levels they had not believed possible. This capacity to "hear each other to speech" is the key to creating communities of discourse that can help us deepen the identity and integrity from which good teaching comes.

Of course, there are less dramatic and less demanding ways to change the ground rules of conversation—the clearness committee is not the method of choice in every situation! But precisely because of its drama, this model can heighten our awareness of why the rules need changing, of what those changes might look like, and of the opportunities for community we lose by acceding to conventional conversational norms.

THE NEED FOR LEADERSHIP

When we talk about leadership, we have a tendency to contrast *communities,* which are supposed to be leaderless, with *institutions,* which need leaders. But it is possible to argue the opposite. Institutions can survive for a while without a leader simply by following bureaucratic rules. But community is a dynamic state of affairs that demands leadership at every turn.

Community does not emerge spontaneously from some relational reflex, especially not in the complex and often conflicted institutions where most teachers work. If we are to have communities of discourse about teaching and learning—communities that are intentional about the topics to be pursued and the ground rules to be practiced—we need leaders who can call people toward that vision.

Good talk about good teaching is unlikely to happen if presidents and principals, deans and department chairs, and others who have influence without position do not *expect* it and *invite* it into being. Those verbs are important because leaders who try to coerce conversation will fail. Conversation must be a free choice—but in the privatized academy, conversation begins only as leaders invite us out of isolation into generative ways of using our freedom.

This kind of leadership can be defined with some precision: it involves offering people excuses and permissions to do things that they want to do but cannot initiate themselves. I can best illustrate what I mean by stepping, for a moment, outside of the academy.

I once worked as a community organizer in a suburb that had been largely white and was becoming racially diverse. Some of the long-term white residents were resistant to this change, and a few signs of overt racism had appeared. My colleagues and I, along with other, more established community leaders, needed to find a way to point the community toward a vision of pluralism in which the promise out-weighs the threat.

Like many organizers, I was schooled in a style of leadership based on allies and enemies: find your allies and make common cause with them, then use your collective power to marginalize and defeat the enemy. But as I came to know this community, I discovered a hopeful fact: not all of the white residents were the enemy.

Many of them had fled from racial diversity at least once before in their lives. Weary of running, they understood that there is no place left to run, and they were looking for ways to accept diversity and find the best in their changing situation. Indeed, some of them had a vision of pluralism's possibilities far more positive than they had been given credit for.

However resistant they seemed on the surface—or in stereo-type—many of these people wanted to find a way to make their com-munity work. They had an "enlightened self-interest" in believing in pluralism's potentials. If they could cultivate that belief and work toward positive ends, they would no longer need to exhaust them-selves running toward an isolationist mirage.

What we needed, as organizers, was not an allies-versus-enemies strategy based on surface fears, for that would only become a self-fulfilling prophecy. We needed a strategy built on people's deeper, unarticulated hopes, offering them excuses and permissions to do what they wanted to do but did not know how to do for themselves.

Of all the excuses and permissions we offered, one of the most effective was a community survey. We knew that fear fades when people meet the stranger and learn not only that the stranger lacks horns but may even come bearing gifts. So we believed that the older residents would be less anxious about the future if they could knock on a newcomer's door, introduce themselves, extend a welcome, and ask how things were going. Yet asking most people to do such a thing is like asking them to fly to the moon.

Under the guise of gathering data about the community, we re-cruited old-timers from churches and synagogues to go out with clip-boards and questionnaires in hand. Their assignment was to knock on a newcomer's door, introduce themselves, extend a welcome, and ask how things were going—with a series of questions to be an-swered on a five-point scale! Putting people in the role of researchers, with clipboards and questionnaires, gave them the excuse and permission they needed to do the most ordinary thing in the world: meet their neighbors.

When the poll takers returned, the data they delivered had intrinsic value. But they brought back something far more valuable: face-to-face contact with other human beings, and stories about the people they had met: "She has the cutest kids"; "They wanted to learn more about our church"; "It turns out he's involved in Little League too." These encounters and stories energized the religious community to raise enough money to launch a foundation, whose programs gave the community new opportunities to weave itself together.

My story may seem far afield from education, but it makes an important point about the kind of leadership education needs. If leaders are to help create good talk about good teaching, they need to discern the difference between what faculty sometimes say about themselves and what their real needs are. Then leaders must provide excuses and permissions to allow the real needs to be met.

Some faculty speak as if they value neither teaching nor talking about teaching. Research and publication, involvement in their professional guilds, dialogue with scholars in their fields—these are the important things. Teaching, they say, is a necessary chore, the price one pays for a chance to pursue one's scholarship, so opportunities to develop their teaching that require more than minimal time and energy are unlikely to appeal to these scholars.

Though this is the way some faculty talk, I do not believe it is the whole truth about all of them, any more than I believed that resistance to diversity was the whole truth about the people in the community I worked with. I believe that many faculty attach much meaning to teaching—so much that when teaching does not go well, they adopt a protective self-alienation.

Yes, many faculty invest heavily in professional activities outside of classrooms. But many spend a considerable part of their lives inside those rooms, so they have an enlightened self-interest in making the most of that part. Some of them have an even more compelling self-interest in connecting meaningfully with the lives of the young, in choosing generativity rather than stagnation.

Leadership in the academy means looking behind the masks we wear and perceiving our true condition. It means seeing more in teachers than teachers sometimes see in themselves—just as good teachers see more in students than students know they have. It means offering permissions and excuses for faculty who want to enrich their experience as teachers but do not know how to do so for themselves.

Some of those permissions are commonplace today. On many campuses, leaders hold an annual workshop that gives faculty an excuse to talk about teaching and learning—a good start, but not nearly enough. In a growing number of places, leaders have created teaching and learning centers that serve the same purposes as the annual workshop but with more constancy and cumulative effect. These structures have great potential, as long as significant topics are addressed under ground rules that encourage authentic dialogue.

I have seen other, less common forms of permission that could be replicated on many campuses. One college has established the position of "teaching consultant." It is occupied each year by a respected teacher on the faculty who is given a reduced course load during his or her year in office.

The job has two parts. The first is simply to be available to colleagues who seek help with their teaching, whether in developing a syllabus, dealing with an immediate crisis, or wanting a classroom observer who can reflect with them on their practice. The second is to sense what is happening on campus that bears on teaching and learning and to provide occasions, from informal coffee hours to formal workshops, where teachers, among themselves or with students, can discuss their concerns.

The institutional investment in such a position is relatively small, but its payoff can be great. The simple fact that a respected colleague has agreed to say, "Let's talk," if I walk into his or her office with a concern about my teaching, gives me the permission to do what I need to do.

Another college has figured out how to get colleagues into each other's classes as more than casual observers without burdening the lives of busy people. In the middle of a course and again toward the end, a colleague I have selected comes into my classroom for half an hour or so, and I take my leave. This colleague—who has talked with me about my concerns and hopes for the course—conducts an open interview with the students about how things are going, an interview in which he or she not only asks questions and gets answers but also probes for nuance, complexity, and detail. Afterward, my colleague sits down with me and helps me sort through the student responses.

This approach not only gives colleagues a way to tap into each other's teaching but also puts them in dialogue with the student experience. Furthermore, it gives students a voice more vivid and nuanced than a questionnaire allows, because their true feelings can be elicited through sensitive interviewing. Finally, it requires that students listen to each other, an action that might reframe their experience: the student in the back row who cannot abide the course must listen to the one in front who finds it a life-changing experience.

Yet another college has found a way to engage students even more deeply in good talk about good teaching. Here, students are trained to be participant-observers in classes they are not taking for credit; their credits, and their grades, come from an education class in which they learn how to observe and evaluate what is happening in a classroom.

Every week or two, the student sits down with the professor of the class being observed. The student can talk about how it feels to be a taking that class—either from a personal standpoint or from what is being said on the grapevine. The student can comment on the process ("You seem to make eye contact with just a few students") and on substantive issues as well ("You might want to revisit the point you were making today—I don't think everyone got it"). Some professors find this dialogue so valuable that they actively seek the participant-observer's help: "What do you think happened yesterday when we had that conflict in class?" or "Any suggestions about how I can make the transition to the next topic without losing the students who still don't understand the last one?"

Good talk about good teaching can take many forms and involve many conversation partners—and it can transform teaching and learning. But it will happen only if leaders expect it, invite it, and provide hospitable space for the conversation to occur. Leaders who work this way understand that good leadership sometimes takes the form of teaching. They lead from the same model we have been exploring for teaching itself, creating a space centered on the great thing called teaching and learning around which a community of truth can gather.

Becoming a leader of that sort—one who opens, rather than occupies, space—requires the same inner journey we have been exploring for teachers. It is a journey beyond fear and into authentic selfhood, a journey toward respecting otherness and understanding how connected and resourceful we all are. As those inner qualities deepen, the leader becomes better able to open spaces in which people feel invited to create communities of mutual support.

Such community is not easily achieved in academic life, given all that divides us. It is most likely to happen when leaders call us back to the heart of teaching and learning, to the work we share and to the shared passion behind that work. If we can create such communities of collegial discourse, they could offer more than support in the development of work-related skills—they could offer healing for the pain of disconnection from which many faculty suffer these days.

In the quotation at the head of this chapter, from *The Once and Future King,* Merlyn speaks in his role as mentor to Arthur, a leader in the making, and offers him a cure for his sadness and pain. It is worth reading again, for the pathologies it names are so familiar to anyone who knows faculty life, and the cure it prescribes is no more or less than the mission of education:

> "The best thing for being sad," replied Merlyn . . . "is to learn
> something. That is the only thing that never fails. You may grow
> old and trembling in your anatomies, you may lie awake at night
> listening to the disorder of your veins, . . . you may see the world
> around you devastated by evil lunatics, or know your honor
> trampled in the sewers of baser minds. There is only one thing for
> it then—to learn. Learn why the world wags and what wags it.
> That is the only thing which the mind can never exhaust, never
> alienate, never be tortured by, never fear or distrust, and never
> dream of regretting. Learning is the thing for you."[2]

If we who lead and we who teach would take that counsel to heart, everyone in education, administrators and teachers and students alike, would have a chance at healing and new life. Learning—learning together—is the thing for all of us.

Chapter VII

Divided No More
Teaching from a Heart of Hope

It goes on one at a time,
it starts when you care
to act, it starts when you do
it again after they said no,
it starts when you say We
and know who you mean, and each
day you mean one more.

—MARGE PIERCY, "THE LOW ROAD"[1]

GRIDLOCK, DESPAIR, AND HOPE

The focus in this final chapter shifts from the practice of teaching to the question of educational reform: Is it possible to embody our best insights about teaching and learning in a social movement that might revitalize education?

The question is more than theoretical for me—it emerges from a personal dilemma. As I travel the country talking with teachers about their practice, I meet many people who care about education and who have compelling visions for change. But after we have talked for a while, the conversation often takes a discouraging turn.

No matter how hopeful our dialogue has been, no matter how many of our colleagues have embraced a new vision, no matter how many practical possibilities we have explored, someone will say, "These are wonderful ideas, but every last one of them will be defeated by the conditions in my school."

That claim is followed by a litany of institutional impediments to reform: a president or dean who understands business better than education; course loads so heavy or classes so large that quality cannot be maintained; an institutional reward system that claims to value teaching but promotes only professors who publish; the flow of scarce dollars away from teaching toward administration or research or bricks and mortar.

When I sense the despair some faculty feel as they talk about these forces, it is hard not to share it. So I have been forced to ask myself whether the pessimists are right. If they are, integrity would require me to stop peddling false hope about the renewal of teaching and learning.

Grant, for the moment, that institutions are as powerful and resistant as the pessimists say they are. The question then becomes, "Has significant social change ever been achieved in the face of massive institutional opposition?" The answer seems clear: *only* in the face of such opposition has significant social change been achieved. If institutions had a capacity for constant evolution, there would never have been a crisis demanding transformation.

The counterpoint to institutional resistance takes the form of social movements, which are the focus of this chapter. But before I polarize the discussion and pit movements against organizations (thus lapsing into another either-or), I want to celebrate the paradoxical relation of the two, affirming the both-and symbiosis that a healthy society requires.

Organizations and movements both play creative roles, but to quite different ends. Organizations represent the principle of order and conservation: they are the vessels in which a society holds hard-won treasures from the past. Movements represent the principle of flux and change: they are the processes through which a society channels its energies for renewal and transformation. A healthy society will encourage interplay between the two. Reform-minded organizational leaders will often welcome movement energies, despite the chaos they can bring, and leaders of movements must understand that they need organizational structures to sustain whatever reforms they may achieve.

But when organizational assumptions are imposed on problems that require movement sensibilities, because organizations are thought to define the limits within which social change can happen, the outcome is often despair. Now the question becomes, "How can the power contained within the structures of this organization be rearranged or redirected to achieve the desired goal?" It is a good question—when asked in context. But it is a bad question when it assumes that organizations are the only game in town. In this scenario, fragile and untested visions of change, harbored by a minority of individuals, are pitted against massive and entrenched patterns of corporate power, and the reform game is lost before it begins.

Constrained by organizational assumptions, people with visions for change expend their energies trying to persuade the authorities to see things another way. If it works, it is a fine strategy. But it often backfires: the authorities withhold their blessing, the visionaries feel betrayed, and an energy sink of resentment is all that remains. When organizations prove to be less interested in change than in preserving the prevailing order—which is, after all, their job—reformers are likely to jump ship and sink in a sea of despond if the organizational approach to change is the only one they know.

But there is another way—the way of the movement. My understanding of movements began with an observation and a question: many people give up in the face of institutional resistance, but others seem to find in that resistance a source of energy for the campaign. Why?

I began to see that there is a "movement mentality," in which resistance is received as the place where everything begins, not ends. In this mentality, not only does change happen in spite of institutional resistance, but resistance helps change happen. The resistance itself points to the need for something new. It encourages us to imagine alternatives. And it energizes those who are called to work toward those ends.

The civil rights and women's movements would have died aborning if racist and sexist organizations had been allowed to define both the battleground and the rules of engagement. But some minorities and some women performed an inner alchemy on organizational resistance, transforming it from social discouragement and defeat to personal inspiration and power. In both of these movements, advocates of change used organizational resistance as a trampoline to spring themselves free of organizations. They found sources of countervailing power outside of those structures, then consolidated that power in ways that eventually gave them leverage on the structures themselves.

The genius of social movements is paradoxical: they abandon the logic of organizations so that they can gather the momentum necessary to alter the logic of organizations. Both the civil rights and women's movements had to free themselves from racist and sexist organizations in order to generate power. Then, with that power, they returned to change the lay, and the law, of the land.

If we want a movement for educational reform, we must learn to embrace this paradox. We must also learn the logic of a movement, learn how a movement unfolds, partly so that we can know where we are located within it, partly so that we can help it along. In the movements I have studied—the civil rights movement; the women's movement; the movements for freedom in eastern Europe, South Africa, and Latin America; and the movement for gay and lesbian rights—I see four definable stages of development.

As with any such model, all of these stages are ideal types. They do not unfold as neatly as the model suggests: they overlap, circle back, and sometimes play leapfrog with each other. But by naming them, however abstractly, we can distill the essential dynamics of a movement from its chaotic energy field:

Stage 1. Isolated individuals make an inward decision to live *"divided no more,"* finding a center for their lives outside of institutions.

Stage 2. These individuals begin to discover one another and form *communities of congruence* that offer mutual support and opportunities to develop a shared vision.

Stage 3. These communities start *going public,* learning to convert their private concerns into the public issues they are and receiving vital critiques in the process.

Stage 4. A system of *alternative rewards* emerges to sustain the movement's vision and to put pressure for change on the standard institutional reward system.

I want to examine each of these stages, but not merely in remembrance of things past. By understanding how movements work, we may discover that we are already actors in a movement for educational reform. We may discover that if one is on an inner journey, one is on the threshold of real power—the power of personal authenticity that, manifested in social movements, has driven real change in our own time. When we know that such power is within our reach, we may be less tempted to succumb to organizational gridlock, less tempted to indulge ourselves in the sweetness of despair.

An Undivided Life

The starting point of a movement, though silent and barely visible, can be described with some precision. It happens when isolated individuals who suffer from a situation that needs changing decide to live "divided no more." These people come to a juncture where they must choose between allowing selfhood to die or claiming the identity and integrity from which good living, as well as good teaching, comes.

Many of us know from personal experience how it feels to live a divided life. Inwardly, we experience one imperative for our lives, but outwardly we respond to quite another. This is the human condition, of course—our inner and outer worlds are never in perfect harmony. But there are extremes of dividedness that become intolerable, when one can no longer live without bringing one's actions into harmony with one's inner life. When that happens inside of one person, then another, and another, and another, in relation to a significant social issue, a movement may be conceived.

The condition to be overcome by living divided no more has a specific etiology. We inhabit institutional settings, including school and work and civic society, because they harbor opportunities that we value. But the claims those institutions make on us are sometimes at odds with our hearts—for example, the demand for loyalty to the corporation, right or wrong, versus the inward imperative to speak truth. That tension can be creative, up to a point. It becomes pathological when the heart becomes a wholly owned subsidiary of the organization, when we internalize organizational logic and allow it to overwhelm the logic of our own lives.

To live divided no more is to find a new center for one's life, a center external to the institution and its demands. This does not mean leaving the institution physically; one may stay at one's post. But it does mean taking one's spiritual leave. One finds solid ground on which to stand outside the institution—the ground of one's own being—and from that ground is better able to resist the deformations that occur when organizational values become the landscape of one's inner life.

The decision to live an undivided life, made by enough people over a long enough period of time, may eventually have social and political impact. But this is not a strategic decision, taken to achieve some political goal. It is a deeply personal decision, made for the sake of one's own identity and integrity. To decide to live divided no more is less a strategy for attacking other people's beliefs than an uprising of the elemental need for one's own beliefs to govern and guide one's life. The power of an authentic movement lies in the fact that it originates in naming and claiming one's identity and integrity—rather than accusing one's "enemies" of lacking the same.

I call this the Rosa Parks decision, for she is our most vivid icon of the undivided life. Indeed, she is an icon we must continue to hold before us, for the movement she sparked still has far to go. On December 1, 1955, in Montgomery, Alabama, Rosa Parks decided to live divided no more—decided that she could no longer act as if she were less than a full human being, the way institutional racism had defined her. She decided that she must act instead on her heart's knowledge of her own humanity. So she did a simple thing: she sat down in the whites-only front section of a segregated bus and refused to yield her seat to a white man.

Rosa Parks had prepared herself for this moment. She had studied strategies of nonviolence at the Highlander Folk School and had served as secretary of the Montgomery chapter of the National Association for the Advancement of Colored People (NAACP). Her act precipitated a public transportation boycott led by Martin Luther King Jr., resulting in a federal court decision that bus segregation laws were unconstitutional and giving impetus to the civil rights movement.

But when great moments in history are reconstructed with the intentionality that comes only with hindsight, we forget the lone individual in the moment of her decision and the anxiety or doubt she may have felt. And when we forget that, we forget our own power.

Myles Horton, founder of the Highlander Folk School, tells about the time he introduced Rosa Parks to Eleanor Roosevelt:

Mrs. Roosevelt asked . . . , "Have you been called a Communist yet, Mrs. Parks?" When Rosa answered yes, Mrs. Roosevelt said, "I suppose Myles told you when you were at Highlander that you'd be called a Communist." Rosa told her I hadn't warned her, and Mrs. Roosevelt criticized me for [that]. I said, "If I'd known what she was going to do, I'd have told her. But when she was at Highlander, she said she wasn't going to do anything. She said that . . . the white people wouldn't let the black people do anything, and besides, the black people hadn't been willing to stick together, so she didn't think she'd do anything. I didn't see any reason to tell a person who wasn't going to do anything that she'd be branded as a Communist. . . . If I'd known she was going to start the civil rights movement, I'd have told her." And Rosa said, "Yes, he told me later on, after I got arrested."[2]

Obviously, Rosa Parks overcame her own doubts and decided to act. But she did so with no guarantees that her training would pay off, that nonviolent strategies would work, that her colleagues would share the risk with her, or that she would spark a national uprising. In fact, other people had committed similar acts with no results except punishment. Had Rosa Parks sat there calculating the odds of making history, she might well have moved to the back of the bus. The decision she made was rooted in the only sure place we have, no matter how shaky we feel: the deep inwardness of an integrity that tells us we must do this thing.

Why did Rosa Parks stay in her seat that day? The best answer comes in her own words: "People always say that I didn't give up my seat because I was tired, but that isn't true. I was not tired physically, or no more tired than I usually was at the end of a working day. I was not old, although some people have an image of me as being old then. I was forty-two. No, the only tired I was, was tired of giving in."[3]

With these words Rosa Parks calls us to the simple, nonstrategic humanity of her act. She was simply tired, tired in her heart and in her soul, tired not only of racism but of her own complicity in the diminishing effects of racism, tired of all the times she had yielded her seat to whites, tired of the self-inflicted suffering her collaboration had brought on.

Concealed in that analysis is a truth about movements that is often ignored: in deciding to live divided no more, the individual goes beyond criticizing an institution and becomes self-critical as well. By choosing an undivided life, I implicitly acknowledge that the institution would not have had power over me if I had refused to go along with it. No longer are "those people" or "that place" my immediate problem. My immediate problem is me and the silent conspiracy I have had with the institution, the conspiracy that allowed that institution to rule my life.

To choose the undivided life is to put flesh on the Pogo principle: "We has met the enemy, and it is us." The moment we decide to stop being our own enemy, we free ourselves from institutional constraints and gain power to confront the institution. But here I must speak with care about the relation of movements to institutions.

We think of movements as hatefully and self-righteously hammering away at evil structures until the structures fall—and we contrast them, often invidiously, with the "slow, steady, responsible" process of caring for an institution and working for change from within. But that portrayal can easily be reversed. People who confine themselves to organizational infighting often become obsessed with internal enemies and possessed by the demons of institutions. People who start movements do so not because they hate an institution but because they love it too much to let it descend to its lowest form.

That is how Rosa Parks felt about the institution of American democracy that had permitted racism to flourish. Democracy was not to be despised and replaced with some fantasy of raceless totalitarianism; it was to be rescued from its degradations and called back to its highest purposes. Having recognized that the enemy is not simply "out there" but first and foremost "in here," in our personal collaboration with evil, Rosa Parks was able to act from love rather than hate—the love that wants to redeem the enemy that can be found in us as well as around us.

What does all of this have to do with educational reform? As I have understood the nature of movements more clearly, I have realized that I meet teachers around the country who remind me of Rosa Parks: they love education too much to let it sink to its lowest form, and—whether they know it or not—they are sparking a movement for educational reform by deciding to live divided no more.

These teachers remember the passions that led them to become academics, and they do not want to lose the primal energy of their vocation. They affirm their deep caring for the lives of students, and they do not want to disconnect from the young. They understand the identity and integrity that they have invested in teaching, and they want to reinvest, even if it pays no institutional interest or dividends.

These teachers have decided that teaching is a front-of-the-bus thing for them, even though their institutions want it moved to the back. They have stopped blaming institutional conditions for teaching's low estate and have stopped conspiring with those conditions as well. Instead, they act in ways that honor their own commitment to the importance of teaching. What these teachers do is often as simple as refusing to yield their seat on the bus: they teach each day in ways that honor their own deepest values rather than in ways that conform to the institutional norm. Sometimes they take risks of a more public sort, promoting alternative visions of education in faculty forums where pedagogical policy is made.

What drives the decision to live divided no more, with the risks it entails? How do people find the courage to bring inner conviction into harmony with outer act, knowing that when they do, the force of the institution may come down on their heads, risking the loss of image or status or security or money or power? The difference between the person who goes to the back of the bus and one who decides to sit up front is probably lost in the mystery of the human heart. But in Rosa Parks and others like her, I see a clue to an answer: when you realize that you can no longer collaborate in something that violates your own integrity, your understanding of punishment is suddenly transformed.

When the police came to Rosa Parks on the bus and informed her that they would have to put her in jail if she did not move, she replied, "You may do that."[4] It was a very polite way of saying, "How could your jail begin to compare with the jail I have had myself in all these years by collaborating with this racist system?"

The courage to live divided no more, and to face the punishment that may follow, comes from this simple insight: *no punishment anyone lays on you could possibly be worse than the punishment you lay on yourself by conspiring in your own diminishment.* With that insight comes the ability to open cell doors that were never locked in the first place and to walk into new possibilities that honor the claims of one's heart.

The decision to live an undivided life, however powerful its motivation, is at first a frail reed. It needs continual reinforcement because the person who makes it soon begins to feel anxiety and self-doubt—naturally so, for we live in a culture that tells us a divided life is sane but an undivided life is foolish at best and irresponsible at worst.

The undivided life is foolish because if you let others know what is going on inside, they may reject and injure you, so it is better to keep your feelings tucked away. It is irresponsible because if you reveal your inner truth, you can no longer perform your duties dispassionately—duties like teaching from a detached, "objective" stance—so it is better to play your role and keep personal truth hidden away.

In the second stage of a movement, people who have chosen the undivided life but still feel shaky about it come together in communities of congruence whose first purpose is simply mutual reassurance. In company with others who are on the same path, these people are helped to understand that "normal" behavior can be crazy but that seeking integrity is always sane.

In the movement sparked by Rosa Parks, these communities of congruence found a home in the black churches. Throughout the South, churches served as gathering places for people who needed to know that they were not alone in choosing an integral life. But the churches offered more than physical space where people could meet. They offered conceptual space where the substance of the movement could be developed and sustained.

Here is the second function of communities of congruence: to help people develop the language that can represent the movement's vision, giving that language the strength it will need to survive and thrive in the rough-and-tumble of the public realm. When discourse begins among people who have recently freed their souls, the language feels fragile—the fragility that comes when we talk about dreams in a society obsessed with practicality or about community in a society obsessed with competition or about risk taking in a society obsessed with playing it safe. People who use such language, the language of the heart, need a place to practice it, to grow accustomed to it, to have it affirmed by like-minded people before they speak it to a larger audience that may range from skeptical to hostile.

When Martin Luther King Jr. went to that larger audience with images of his "dream" or the "mountaintop," he was drawing on a reservoir of symbols that had been tapped time and again in this movement's communities of congruence. Such images were not the private property of King, the great orator. They were the lingua franca of ordinary people; through constant use in the black churches, they had gained accessibility and power.

Those churches played a third role characteristic of communities of congruence: they provided a training ground where people living undivided lives could develop the skills and habits necessary to take their values into the larger world. I once had a vivid experience of this. I was visiting a community in rural Georgia and was invited to worship with a small African American congregation. I arrived in time to attend the adult Sunday school class and found myself in a room with three other people who were preparing to discuss a Bible passage. To my surprise, they ran their class by *Robert's Rules of Order,* and each of them had a role to play: one was the chairperson, one was the secretary, and one was the parliamentarian.

Afterward, I shared my puzzlement with the friend who had taken me to church, himself a resident of the area and a frequent attendee. Why had the class practiced such formality when there were only three people present? Wouldn't it make more sense just to sit and talk?

He said, "You don't understand what you just saw. This church is a place where people who have been deprived of a role in governing our society have a chance to learn some tools of governance. Someday these people will claim their rightful role, and when they do, they'll have the capacity to perform it."

Communities of congruence are vital in educational reform, but creating them is made difficult by the privatization of academic life. I am often reminded of this fact when I visit a campus for two or three days. When my opening talk is over, someone will come up to me and confide, "I agree with everything you say about teaching— but I am the only person on campus who feels this way." At the end of the second session, three or four more people will approach me, one by one, to share the same secret.

By the time I leave, I have met ten or fifteen people who share a common vision for education—each of whom is certain that he or she is alone on this campus. More than once I have tried to introduce those people to one another, hoping to plant the seeds of a community of congruence that might take root and grow in that place. Such communities emerge when two or three people gather and make a commitment to each other. I have seen this happening especially among women in academia, who are engaged in two movements at once—one for good teaching, another for the place of women in the academy.

But if communities of congruence are to develop on a significant scale, they may require structural support. Black churches provided that support in the civil rights movement—they were standing structures that embraced a large and concerned constituency, built on a system of symbols that provided a rhetoric of liberation. Are there structures in the academy that could shelter communities of congruence for teachers who want to live divided no more?

There are no standing structures with the credibility and power of the black churches, but that does not mean that the game is lost. I am aware of at least two educational structures that have some movement potentials and are already serving such purposes, however modestly. One is the growing number of "teaching and learning centers" on campuses large and small. The programs at these centers often focus on training in technique for faculty who want it or need it. In the process—sometimes intentionally, sometimes not—these centers offer committed teachers a place to find each other, talk with each other, and discover ways to provide each other with continuing support.

A second structure is the growing number of regional and national associations that have been organized around the values of deep reform. In the world of higher education, I mean groups like the Association for General and Liberal Studies, the American Association of Higher Education, and the Professional and Organizational Development Network in Higher Education. People who feel isolated on their own campuses can attend gatherings of groups such as these and return home encouraged that they have allies and friends, albeit in distant places.

People involved in movements often have more friends far away than they have at home; the reform agenda that is so inspiring on a national scale turns out to be threatening locally. But when I meet visionary teachers who feel isolated on their own campuses and ask them what they have done to make their vision known, the answer is often nothing—which is why they are isolated. The lost will never be found until they send up a flare.

There is only one way to find friends close to home, one way to plant a seed from which a community of congruence might grow: one must make visible one's decision to live divided no more. Visibility is not easy because it may bring recrimination. But when we declare our values in a visible and viable way, we will sometimes be amazed at the way allies gather round.

GOING PUBLIC

The strength of a movement's second stage is that like-minded people gather in community to reinforce fragile beliefs. But there are two ways in which this strength is also a weakness: when we talk only to each other, and not to a larger audience, no movement can emerge— and we are more likely to fall into delusion and error.

When a movement goes public, not only does it have a chance to influence others with its values but it also meets challenges that compel it to check and correct its values. There is so much "soul force" in making the decision to live an undivided life, and so much reinforcement when people who have made it come together, that the shadow of self-righteousness is almost certain to emerge. The only way to minimize the shadow and maximize the light is to expose the movement to public critique—and to take the critique seriously.

When I explore the movement model with others, it is often criticized for being value-neutral. The model can, for example, describe conservative movements that the critic dislikes as well as liberal movements that he or she applauds. Worse yet, any model that starts with "divided no more" easily applies to fascist movements in which people decide to bring their actions into harmony with the evil that is in their hearts—such as the Nazis, the Ku Klux Klan, and the Aryan Nation.

My first response is that the arena of social change offers no safe harbor for the purity of thought and action so dear to intellectuals.

There are no guarantees that movements will be deployed toward ends I regard as worthy, just as there are no guarantees that organizations will pursue such ends. The life of the world is messy, a source of suffering as well as creativity, and if we want to work for change, we must learn to live with the mess.

But my second response is to make a crucial distinction between a movement, whether I agree with its aims or not, and a pseudo-movement. The distinction hinges on a movement's willingness to enter this third stage and go public. A fascist "movement" refuses to go public—and in that refusal it degenerates from being a movement to being an exercise of coercive power.

The leaders of authentic movements willingly go public and engage in give-and-take, knowing that this public dialogue is a path toward the authority that comes from understanding and persuasion. But in a fascist "movement," the leaders have no interest in public exposure and critique. Indeed, fascism depends on shutting down the public realm so that fascist values cannot be challenged and countervailing power cannot be generated against them.

In a totalitarian society, the public sphere is shut down by main force: no gatherings in public places, no voluntary associations, no free press, no politics worthy of the name. But even in societies like ours, where the public sphere is attenuated but still open, pseudo-movements find ways to evade public scrutiny and accountability. I think, for example, of the radical religious right and its "stealth" candidates who do not reveal their true beliefs until they get elected to public office. Even when the public realm is open, it is possible to evade public scrutiny, at least for a while. But when a group does so, it ceases to be a movement of moral authority and becomes a bald manipulation of power.

When the current movement for educational reform is viewed through the lens of going public, we see that a movement can grow so slowly, so organically, that we are scarcely aware of its impact. Though the movement for educational reform has yet to achieve major goals, the images and symbols of educational reform are alive and well today in the public arena.

Books are written on the subject, and some become best-sellers. Speakers roam the land planting seeds of change in workshops and convocations. New associations advance the cause in national and regional gatherings—and faculty who feel isolated on their own campuses seek them out as oases. Old-line national associations take up the cause as a path toward their own renewal.

Even more important, the movement for educational reform has been joined by publics beyond the walls of the academy. Parents, employers, legislators, and columnists call for more attention to teaching and learning, calls that are insistent and sometimes effective. Here is a case in point from a field not normally regarded as a hotbed of reform, accountancy:

> Many accounting graduates hope for and find initial employment in the "Big Six"—the large, international public accounting firms. These partnerships hire 10,000 graduates each year and donate more than $20 million to support higher education. . . .
>
> In 1989, the CEOs of the top international accounting firms jointly issued a paper detailing what they felt the professional needed from educators. . . . The paper described in some detail the desired knowledge and skills they wanted to see in the graduates they hired [which included the social and cultural context of organizations, creative problem-solving, effective communication, and the ability to work . . . "in groups with diverse members," and the ability to withstand and resolve conflict].
>
> The CEOs' report [stated] . . . , "Passing the CPA Examination should not be the goal of accounting education. The focus should be on developing analytical and conceptual thinking—versus memorizing rapidly expanding professional standards." . . .
>
> In their white paper, the large firms pledged $4 million over five years to help create the changes they sought in the curriculum . . . "contingent on the condition that they be used . . . for the design and implementation of innovative curricula [and] new teaching methods."[5]

When the language of pedagogical reform becomes common coin among the leaders of the Big Six accountancy firms—who then use their considerable clout to press business schools to change—one can see that the movement has made tracks, however quietly and unnoticed.

The way in which the educational reform movement has gone public reveals how untidy reality is, compared to my model of movement stages. For example, educational reform has achieved a scale in

Stage 3 that is disproportionate to the scale of Stage 2: there is more talk about reform in the public realm than one would anticipate from the small number of communities of congruence in the privatized world of traditional education.

But this discrepancy, rather than discrediting the model, shows how valuable models can be, for deviations from the model point us to things that require explanation. Perhaps the discrepancy between Stages 2 and 3 results from the fact that ferment for reform is coming less from teachers in traditional schools than from people who teach in other settings—especially in the world of business and industry, where at least half of the postsecondary education in this country is now being done.

Most major corporations have in-house "universities" to help their employees keep pace with rapid change in society, technology, and markets. For example, each of the Big Six accountancy firms "operates its own education division to provide continuing, graduate-level education to its professional employees. It is not uncommon for a firm to manage over a million contact hours of training each year."[6] Nor is it uncommon for these nontraditional programs to employ pedagogies more inventive than one can find at most colleges and schools.

The energies of this huge sector of nontraditional education could help drive educational reform, if we knew how to harness them. But that will happen only when educators in traditional settings break through their privatization and make common cause with educators from alien worlds. In the words of Marge Piercy, it will start "when you say We/and know who you mean, and each/day you mean one more."[7]

The need for that breakthrough is illustrated by a problem I find on almost every campus I visit. Teachers who use nontraditional methods feel thwarted by the traditionalism of their students, their students' parents, and some of their colleagues: "Stop doing this 'touchy-feely' stuff with students. Cover the field, make them memorize the facts, and show them how to compete. If you don't, you put them at disadvantage in the real world of work."

The irony is clear: the "real" world of work is the source of much pedagogical experimentation and change, precisely because conventional top-down teaching does not prepare students well for the realities of that world. But some students, some parents, and some academics are caught in a cultural lag. They need to hear the news.

Of course, they will not believe the news if it comes only from persons who teach: it must come from authoritative voices in the world of work itself. But many educators, even, and perhaps especially, the most innovative, see people from business and industry as enemies, not allies. We rarely ask, or trust, them to help us to deliver the news that pedagogical change must happen if students are to succeed in the real world.

If we who teach would understand how a movement works and try on a movement mentality, we might find it easier to make common cause with people in the public realm who can help the movement along. Some of them are within easy reach and would gladly join hands with us—they are alumni of our institutions and members of our boards of trustees.

As we seek allies among employers, we will learn that not all of our reservations are unfounded: in the business world, openness to pedagogical reform serves the single purpose of improving the bottom line. Not all our potential allies will understand, let alone honor, the aspirations of the liberal arts, though some clearly do. Not all will subscribe to the central premise of this book that good teaching cannot be reduced to technique, for business is even more enamored of technique than education is.

But making common cause in a movement does not require partners whose vision matches our own. As we link arms, we will find ourselves tugged in dangerous directions, but because our arms are linked, we will have the chance to do some tugging of our own. Making common cause opens the possibility of teaching and learning across previously alien fields.

As a movement goes public, the identity and integrity of its participants are tested against the great diversity of values and visions at work in the public arena. We must stay close to our own integrity in this complex field of forces, where we can easily lose our way. But we must also risk opening ourselves to conflicting influences, for in that way both the movement and our integrity can grow.

The fourth and final stage reveals the full trajectory of those movement energies that were generated in Stage 1, when isolated individuals abandoned the logic of organizations and decided to live divided no more. Those energies—which became communal in Stage 2 and went public in Stage 3—now come back to where they began, returning to alter the logic of the very organizations from which they first sprang free.

I say "alter" rather than "transform" or "revolutionize" the logic of organizations because the outcomes of most movements are modest. They rarely resemble nirvana. Most movements do not overturn the prevailing order but make incremental adjustments to it, on the scale Thomas Merton suggested when he said, "We do not need to adjust to the world; we can adjust the world."[8] Movements are more likely to fine-tune reality than to give rise to a brave new world.

Even more humbling, these modest alterations, once they are institutionalized, eventually become the *ancien régime,* the unbrave old world. They become the shape of the institutional resistance against which the movements of the next generation must press. But they are alterations nonetheless, and if the movement has sound principles, the alterations will also be sound, at least for a while.

Movements have the power to alter the logic of organizations because an organization is, at bottom, a system of social sanctions: do this and you will be punished; do that and you will be rewarded. As long as an institution controls the reward system in a given arena of activity—such as teaching and learning—it has power over the lives of everyone who wants to engage in that activity.

But as soon as those people decide that the institution's punishments are irrelevant (which is the key to Stage 1) and the movement evolves an alternative system of rewards around the activities those people value (which is the key to Stage 4), the institution's power starts to decline. When that happens, institutions often awaken to the need for change, lest the action go elsewhere and they become irrelevant to people's lives.

For example, when virtually all postsecondary education in the United States was done by traditional colleges and universities, those institutions had no need to change. Anyone who wanted to be a student or a teacher was compelled to play by their rules. But now that half or more of our postsecondary education is being done by business, industry, and the military, traditional higher education is feeling the pinch and opening itself to renewal.

What are the alternative rewards that push traditional organizations to rewrite their logic? As a movement grows, it offers intangible but powerful rewards at every stage of development. In Stage 1, there is the reward of learning more about one's identity; in Stage 2, the reward of being in community with supportive and like-minded people; in Stage 3, the reward of living a more expansive public life. As a movement grows, the meaning one is unable to find in working for an institution is found in working for the movement, the affirmation one does not receive from colleagues in one's organization is received from movement friends, and careers that no longer satisfy the soul are redirected toward ends that the movement has inspired.

Movements offer material as well as spiritual rewards. Some people make modest incomes from working for the movement itself, as organizers, for example. Working for the movement can have economic payoffs elsewhere: more than a few academics devoted to educational reform have published books and articles on the movement and its aims that helped earn them promotion or tenure in traditional institutions.

Ultimately, as a movement grows, conventional organizations are more and more likely to create spaces where movement-style work can be done and paid for. Forty years ago, people working openly for racial diversity in the workplace often had a hard time getting paid jobs of any sort. Today, many organizations pay people to be diversity specialists, working for racial and gender harmony and justice among employees. Forty years ago, women and African Americans were often treated as unsuited for scholarly life. Today, black and feminist scholars are often vigorously recruited.

Ultimately, the diverse rewards offered in this final stage of a movement are reflections of the same elemental reward—the reward that comes from living an undivided life. In Stage 1, people see that no punishment anyone lays on them could be worse than the way they punish themselves by conspiring in their own diminishment. In Stage 4, they see that no reward anyone offers them could be greater than the way they reward themselves by living their own truth.

When substantial numbers of people embrace this understanding, institutions are forced to negotiate—for they no longer have a hammerlock on people's hearts.

The alternative rewards offered by a movement may seem fragile compared to the raises, promotions, and status that organizations bestow on loyalists. So they are. Integrity, as the cynics say, does not put bread on the table. But people who are drawn into a movement generally find that stockpiling bread is not the major issue in their lives, not because they have all the bread they want, but because they have a more basic hunger. They understand that human beings do not live by bread alone.

The way of the movement is an alternative to organizational gridlock and the despair it breeds, an alternative with historical precedent and power. But having spent this chapter mapping movements and examining their implications for educational reform, I need to voice a disclaimer: even with map in hand, we may cling to the organizational approach for reasons more sinister than ignorance of another way.

We sometimes get a perverse comfort from insisting that organizations offer the only path toward change. Then, when the path is blocked, as it often is, we can rest in resentment and blame it all on external forces rather than take responsibility ourselves. Part of us prefers being hopeless to taking the risk of new life: if we believed that new life were possible, God knows what we might be called to do! It is not uncommon for academics to be driven by this "death wish," even—and sometimes especially—the most idealistic among us. The most vigorous resistance to the movement option may come from visionaries who have been defeated on one front and are too weary to open another.

I am a teacher at heart, and I am not naturally drawn to the rough-and-tumble of social change. I would sooner teach than spend my energies helping a movement along and taking the hits that come with it. Yet if I care about teaching, I must care not only for my students and my subject but also for the conditions, inner and outer, that bear on the work teachers do. Finding a place in the movement for educational reform is one way to exercise that larger caring.

The four stages of a movement may help us find that place. Some of us may decide to live divided no more, to align our actions as teachers with the meaning we attach to our work. Some of us may seek others who share our values, joining communities of congruence that can sustain our transformation. Some of us may go public with our beliefs, voicing our vision and being challenged by the response. Some of us may learn that conventional rewards pale as we experience the satisfaction of living by our best lights.

As we find our place in the movement, we will discover that there is no essential conflict between loving to teach and working to reform education. An authentic movement is not a play for power— it is teaching and learning writ large. Now the world becomes our classroom, and the potential to teach and learn is found everywhere. We need only be in the world as our true selves, with open hearts and minds.

So we come full circle, to the place where this book began: to the power within each of us that in communion with powers beyond ourselves, co-creates the world, for better or worse. The poet Rumi says, "If you are here unfaithfully with us,/you're causing terrible damage."[9]

The evidence of his claim is all around us, not least in education: when we are unfaithful to the inward teacher and to the community of truth, we do lamentable damage to ourselves, to our students, and to the great things of the world that our knowledge holds in trust.

But Rumi would surely agree that the converse is equally true. If you are here faithfully with us, you are bringing abundant blessing. It is a blessing known to generations of students whose lives have been transformed by people who had the courage to teach—the courage to teach from the most truthful places in the landscape of self and world, the courage to invite students to discover, explore, and inhabit those places in the living of their own lives.

Notes

GRATITUDES

1. For information about the Center for Teacher Formation, please call 1-888-849-4889.

INTRODUCTION

1. Stephen Mitchell (ed.), "Ah, Not to Be Cut Off," in *Ahead of All Parting: The Selected Poetry and Prose of Rainer Maria Rilke* (New York: Modern Library, 1995), p. 191.

CHAPTER I

1. May Sarton, in "Now I Become Myself," *Collected Poems, 1930–1973* (New York: Norton, 1974), p. 156. Copyright © 1993, 1988, 1984, 1947 by May Sarton. Reprinted by permission of W. W. Norton & Company, Inc.
2. Mohandas K. Gandhi, *An Autobiography, or the Story of My Experiments with Truth* (Ahmedabad, India: Navajivan Press, 1927).
3. Cited in Earl Schwartz, "Chronic Life," *Creative Nursing*, Feb. 1992, p. 58.
4. Václav Havel, speech delivered to joint meeting of the U.S. Congress, quoted in *Time*, Mar. 5, 1990, pp. 14–15.
5. Alice Kaplan, *French Lessons: A Memoir* (Chicago: University of Chicago Press, 1993), p. 209.
6. Kaplan, *French Lessons*, pp. 210–211.
7. Kaplan, *French Lessons*, p. 216.
8. C. Wright Mills, *The Sociological Imagination* (New York: Oxford University Press, 1959).

9. Jane Tompkins, "Pedagogy of the Distressed," *College English,* 1991, *52*(6).
10. Florida Scott-Maxwell, *The Measure of My Days* (New York: Penguin Books, 1983), p. 42.
11. Frederick Buechner, *Wishful Thinking: A Seeker's ABC* (San Francisco: HarperSanFrancisco, 1993), p. 119.

CHAPTER II

1. William Stafford, "Lit Instructor," in *Traveling Through the Dark* (New York: HarperCollins, 1962), pp. 77–78. Reprinted by permission of the Estate of William Stafford.
2. Albert Camus, *Notebooks, 1935–1942* (New York: Marlowe, 1996), p. 13.
3. Camus, *Notebooks*, pp. 13–14.
4. Nelle Morton, *The Journey Is Home* (Boston: Beacon Press, 1985), pp. 55–56.
5. Erik H. Erikson, *Identity and the Life Cycle* (New York: Norton, 1964).
6. Alfred North Whitehead, *The Aims of Education* (New York: New American Library/Mentor Books, 1961), p. 13.
7. Karl Pearson, *The Grammar of Science* (London: Dent, 1937), p. 11. My thanks to Mark Schwehn, dean of Christ College at Valparaiso University, for alerting me to this source.
8. Pearson, *The Grammar of Science,* p. 11.
9. Sue V. Rosser, "The Gender Equation," *Sciences,* Sept.-Oct. 1992, p. 46.
10. Evelyn Fox Keller, *A Feeling for the Organism: The Life and Work of Barbara McClintock* (New York: Freeman, 1983), p. 198.
11. Rosser, "The Gender Equation," p. 46.
12. Evelyn Fox Keller, *Reflections on Gender and Science* (New Haven, Conn.: Yale University Press, 1985), p. 164.
13. Stephen Mitchell (ed.), "Ah, Not to Be Cut Off," in *Ahead of All Parting: The Selected Poetry and Prose of Rainer Maria Rilke* (New York: Modern Library, 1995), p. 191.
14. T. S. Eliot, "Little Gidding," in *T. S. Eliot: The Complete Poems and Plays, 1909–1950* (Orlando, Fla.: Harcourt Brace, 1958), p. 145.

CHAPTER III

1. Thomas P. McDonnell (ed.), "Hagia Sophia," in *A Thomas Merton Reader* (New York: Doubleday, 1989), p. 506.
2. These words are attributed to Bohr in many secondary sources (for example, Avery Dulles, *The Reshaping of Catholicism,* [San Francisco: Harper, 1989], p. 37), though I have been unable to find them in his writings. Their authenticity is substantiated by his son, Hans Bohr, in an essay called "My Father": "One of the favorite maxims of my father was the distinction between the two sorts of truths, profound truths recognized by the fact that

the opposite is also a profound truth, in contrast to trivialities where opposites are obviously absurd." S. Rozental (ed.), *Niels Bohr: His Life and Work as Seen by His Friends and Colleagues* (New York: Wiley, 1967), p. 328.

3. Dietrich Bonhoeffer, *Life Together* (New York: HarperCollins, 1954), p. 78.

4. Robert N. Bellah and others, *Habits of the Heart* (Berkeley: University of California Press, 1985).

5. E. F. Schumacher, *Small Is Beautiful: Economics as If People Mattered* (New York: HarperCollins, 1973), pp. 97–98.

6. Rainer Maria Rilke, *Letters to a Young Poet,* M. D. Herter Norton (trans.) (New York: Norton, 1993), p. 35.

7. Florida Scott-Maxwell, *The Measure of My Days* (New York: Penguin Books, 1983), p. 25.

CHAPTER IV

1. Mary Oliver, "Wild Geese," in *Dream Work* (New York: Atlantic Monthly Press, 1986), p. 14.

2. Page Smith, "To Communicate Truth," *Whole Earth Review,* Summer 1987, p. 55.

3. Benjamin Barber, "The Civic Mission of the University," in *Higher Education and the Practice of Democratic Politics,* Bernard Murchland (ed.) (Dayton, Ohio: Kettering Foundation, 1991).

4. Ian Barbour, *Religion in an Age of Science* (San Francisco: HarperSanFrancisco, 1990), p. 107.

5. Barbour, *Religion in an Age of Science.*

6. Gary Zukav, *The Dancing Wu Li Masters* (New York: Morrow, 1979), p. 94.

7. Barbour, *Religion in an Age of Science,* p. 107.

8. Barbour, *Religion in an Age of Science,* p. 220.

9. Barbour, *Religion in an Age of Science,* p. 221.

10. Michael Polanyi, *Personal Knowledge* (Chicago: University of Chicago Press, 1960).

11. Richard Gelwick, "Polanyi: An Occasion of Thanks," *Cross Currents: Religion and Intellectual Life,* 1991, *41,* 380–381. See also Richard Gelwick, *The Way of Discovery: An Introduction to the Thought of Michael Polanyi* (New York: Oxford University Press, 1977).

12. Evelyn Fox Keller, *A Feeling for the Organism: The Life and Work of Barbara McClintock* (New York: Freeman, 1983), p. 200.

13. Robert Frost, "The Secret Sits," from *The Poetry of Robert Frost,* Edward Connery Lathem (ed.) (New York: Henry Holt, 1979), p. 362. Copyright 1942 by Robert Frost, © 1970 by Lesley Frost Ballantine, © 1969 by Henry Holt & Co. Reprinted by permission of Henry Holt and Co., Inc.

14. Oliver, *Dream Work,* p. 14.

15. Keller, *A Feeling for the Organism,* p. 207.
16. James Shapiro, University of Chicago, quoted in "Dr. Barbara McClintock, 90, Gene Research Pioneer Dies," *New York Times,* Sept. 4, 1992, p. C16.
17. Rainer Maria Rilke, *Rodin and Other Prose Pieces* (London: Quartet Books, 1986), p. 4.
18. James D. Watson, *The Double Helix* (New York: Atheneum, 1968).
19. Leon Jaroff, "Happy Birthday, Double Helix," *Time,* Mar. 15, 1993, pp. 58–59.
20. David Denby, *Great Books* (New York: Simon & Schuster, 1996).
21. Annie Dillard, *Teaching a Stone to Talk* (New York: HarperCollins, 1982).
22. A rabbi told me this Hasidic tale. I have not found it in print.
23. Rudolf Otto, *The Idea of the Holy* (London: Oxford University Press, 1952).
24. Hannah Arendt, *Eichmann in Jerusalem: A Report on the Banality of Evil* (New York: Viking Penguin, 1964).
25. Sharon Bertsch McGrayne, *Nobel Prize Women in Science* (New York: Carol, 1993) p. 170.
26. I am grateful to Dawna Markova, scholar and practitioner in the field of bodily knowing, for information about the fight or flight syndrome, "soft eyes," and the practice of aikido. For more on these subjects, see Andy Bryner and Dawna Markova, *An Unused Intelligence* (Berkeley, Calif.: Conari Press, 1996).
27. Diane Ackerman, *A Natural History of the Senses* (New York: Vintage Books, 1991), p. 309.

CHAPTER V

1. David V. Erdman (ed.), "Auguries of Innocence," in *The Complete Poetry and Prose of William Blake* (New York: Doubleday Anchor, 1988), p. 489.
2. "Integrating Community Service and Classroom Instruction Enhances Learning: Results from an Experiment," *Educational Evaluation and Policy Analysis,* 1993, *15,* 410–419.
3. Judith Axler Turner, "Mathematicians Debate Calculus Reform and Better Teaching," *Chronicle of Higher Education,* Jan. 31, 1990, p. A15.
4. "Does Objective Reality Exist, or Is the Universe a Phantasm?" World Wide Web Virtual Library: Sumeria [http://www.livelinks.com/sumeria/].
5. Erdman, *The Complete Poetry and Prose of William Blake,* p. 489.

CHAPTER VI

1. T. H. White, *The Once and Future King* (New York: Ace Books, 1987), p. 183. Reprinted by permission of The Putnam Publishing Group. Copyright © 1939, 1940 by T. H. White; renewed © 1958 by T. H. White Proprietor.
2. T. H. White, *The Once and Future King,* p. 183.

CHAPTER VII

1. Marge Piercy, "The Low Road," in *The Moon Is Always Female* (New York: Knopf, 1981), pp. 44–45. Copyright © 1980 by Marge Piercy. Reprinted by permission of Alfred A. Knopf Inc.
2. Myles Horton, *The Long Haul* (New York: Doubleday, 1990), p. 190.
3. Rosa Parks, *Rosa Parks: My Story* (New York: Dial Books, 1992), p. 116.
4. Parks, *Rosa Parks,* p. 116.
5. Jean C. Wyer, "Accounting Education: Change Where You Might Least Expect It," *Change,* Jan.-Feb. 1993, pp. 15–17.
6. Wyer, "Accounting Education," p. 15.
7. Piercy, *The Moon is Always Female,* pp. 44–45.
8. Personal communication from Brother Patrick Hart, Thomas Merton's personal secretary.
9. Rumi, "Say Yes Quickly," in *Open Secret: Versions of Rumi,* Coleman Brooks (trans.) (Brattleboro, Vt.: Threshold Books, 1984), p. 27.

The Author

Parker J. Palmer is a writer, teacher, and activist who works independently on issues in education, community, leadership, spirituality, and social change. His work spans a wide range of institutions—colleges and universities, public schools, community organizations, religious institutions, corporations, and foundations. He serves as senior associate of the American Association of Higher Education, as senior adviser to the Fetzer Institute, and is the founder of Fetzer's Teacher Formation Program for K–12 teachers.

Palmer travels widely in this country and abroad giving workshops, lectures, and retreats, and has often been cited as a master teacher. His work has been featured by the *New York Times,* the *Chronicle of Higher Education, Change* magazine, *Christian Century,* CBS-TV news, and the Voice of America. The Danforth Foundation, the Lilly Endowment, and the Fetzer Institute have supported his work with major grants. In 1993, he won the national award of the Council of Independent Colleges for Outstanding Contributions to Higher Education. "The Leadership Project," a 1997 survey of 11,000 administrators and faculty by four leading educational associations, named Palmer as one of the nation's most "Influential Leaders in Higher Education."

His writing has been recognized with four honorary doctorates, two Distinguished Achievement Awards from the National

Educational Press Association, Critic's Choice citations from *Commonweal* and *Christian Century* magazines, selection by several book clubs, and translation into several languages. His publications include ten poems, some eighty essays, and several widely used books, including *The Promise of Paradox, The Company of Strangers, To Know As We Are Known,* and *The Active Life.*

Palmer received the B.A. degree in philosophy and sociology from Carleton College, where he was elected to Phi Beta Kappa and was awarded a Danforth Graduate Fellowship. After a year at Union Theological Seminary, he studied sociology at the University of California at Berkeley, where he received the M.A. and Ph.D. degrees with honors. He lives in Madison, Wisconsin.

Courage to Teach Program

Under the guidance of Parker J. Palmer, the Fetzer Institute created Courage to Teach, a seasonal program of quarterly retreats for the personal and professional renewal of public school educators. The retreat program primarily serves K–12 educators, administrators, and educational leaders on whom our society depends for so much but for whom we provide so little.

Courage to Teach employs an approach to vocational renewal called "formation." The formation process invites educators to reclaim their own wholeness and vocational clarity and makes connections between the renewal of a teacher's spirit and the revitalization of public education. This approach to personal and professional renewal is rooted in the belief that good teaching flows from the identity and integrity of the teacher.

The Center for Teacher Formation was established in 1997 to develop, deepen, and expand the work of teacher formation nationally. The center provides information and consultation to individuals and communities that wish to initiate Courage to Teach programs. The center is also responsible for the selection and preparation of formation facilitators.

For more information about the Center for Teacher Formation and Courage to Teach, please see our Web site: www.teacherformation.org

Index

medical school, 124–128;
metaphors and images of,
147–150; from microcosm,
120–132; and open space,
132–135; paradox in, 61–87; in
social research, 128–132; subject-centered, 115–120; tangles
of, 2; and technique, 5–6, 9–13,
24, 32–33
Tennyson, A., 95
Tompkins, J., 28–29, 186
Total Quality Management, 93
Troeltsch, E., 137
Truth: community of, 90, 95, 97,
99–106, 115–116, 120–122,
126–128, 134–135, 138, 141;
concept of, 104; models of,
100–102; as nonlinear, 134–135

Turner, J. A., 188

V

Vietnam, war in, 53
Vocation, and gladness, 30

W

Watson, J. D., 108, 188
Weber, M., 137
White, T. H., 141, 188
Whitehead, A. N., 52, 186
Wholeness, hidden, and paradox,
61–87
Women's movement, 165–166
Wyer, J. C., 189

Z

Zukav, G., 187

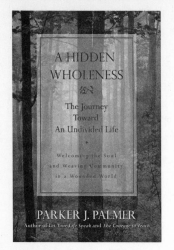

A Hidden Wholeness: The Journey Toward an Undivided Life

Parker J. Palmer

$22.95 Hardcover ISBN: 0787971006

A BookSense Pick, September 2004

This book is a treasure an inspiring, useful blueprint for building safe places where people can commit to "act in every situation in ways that honor the soul."— *Publishers Weekly*

"The soul is generous: it takes in the needs of the world. The soul is wise: it suffers without shutting down. The soul is hopeful: it engages the world in ways that keep opening our hearts. The soul is creative: it finds a path between realities that might defeat us and fantasies that are mere escapes. All we need to do is to bring down the wall that separates us from our own soul and deprives the world of the souls regenerative powers."—From *A Hidden Wholeness*

At a time when many of us seek ways of working and living that are more resonant with our souls, *A Hidden Wholeness* offers insight into our condition and guidance for finding what we seek within ourselves and with each other.

PARKER J. PALMER is a highly respected writer, lecturer, teacher, and activist. His work speaks deeply to people from many walks of life, including public schools, college and universities, religious institutions, corporations, foundations, and grassroots organizations. The Leadership Project, a 1998 survey of 10,000 American educators, named him one of the thirty most influential senior leaders in higher education and one of ten key "agenda-setters" of the past decade. Author of six previous books including the best-sellers *Let Your Life Speak* and *The Courage to Teach* his writing has been recognized with eight honorary doctorates and several national awards. He holds a Ph.D. from the University of California at Berkley and lives in Madison, Wisconsin.

[Price subject to change]

Let Your Life Speak:
Listening for the Voice of Vocation
Parker J. Palmer

$18.00 Hardcover ISBN: 0787947350

Parker Palmer's writing is like a high country stream—clear, vital, honest. If your life seems to be passing you by, or you cannot see the way ahead, immerse yourself in the wisdom of these pages and allow it to carry you toward a more attentive relationship with your deeper, truer self.—JOHN S. MOGABGAB, editor, *Weavings Journal*

"Is the life I am living the same as the life that wants to live in me?" With this searching question, Parker J. Palmer begins an insightful and moving meditation on finding one's true calling. *Let Your Life Speak* is an openhearted gift to anyone who seeks to live authentically. The book's title is a time-honored Quaker admonition, usually taken to mean "Let the highest truths and values guide everything you do." But Palmer reinterprets those words, drawing on his own search for selfhood. "Before you tell your life what you intend to do with it," he writes, "listen for what it intends to do with you. Before you tell your life what truths and values you have decided to live up to, let your life tell you what truths you embody, what values you represent."

Vocation does not come from willfulness, no matter how noble one's intentions. It comes from listening to and accepting "true self" with its limits as well as its potentials. Sharing stories of frailty and strength, of darkness and light, Palmer shows that vocation is not a goal to be achieved but a gift to be received. A compassionate and compelling meditation on discovering your path in life with wisdom, compassion, and gentle humor, Parker J. Palmer invites us to listen to the inner teacher and follow it toward a sense of meaning and purpose.

PARKER J. PALMER is a highly respected writer who works independently on issues in education, community, spirituality, and social change; he offers lectures, workshops, and retreats across the country. He has inspired a generation of teachers and reformers with evocative visions of community, knowing, and spiritual wholeness. He lives in Madison, Wisconsin.

[Price subject to change]

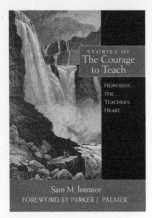

Stories of the Courage to Teach: Honoring the Teacher's Heart

Sam M. Intrator

$23.95 Hardcover   ISBN: 0787956325

Stories of the Courage to Teach: Honoring the Teacher's Heart *powerfully reminds us that this nation's schools and colleges are blessed with many good teachers and that we must be willing to respect, support, and deeply listen to them. It also indicates that teachers must also learn to listen to themselves. Our history books are filled with examples of the efforts of committed education employees who helped to make this country what it is today.* Stories of the Courage to Teach *challenges today's teachers to see themselves not only as school employees, dedicated to serving children, but as leaders in their schools and communities.*
—Bob Chase, president, National Teachers Association

This moving collection of stories is written by real teachers struggling to reconnect with the source of their vocation. It offers much-needed encouragement to the hearts of teachers and includes practical depictions of what can—and does—go on in an enlivened classroom. *Stories of the Courage to Teach* draws its inspiration from Parker Palmer's best-selling *The Courage to Teach,* the book that dared to reach out to teachers across America who have been too long underestimated, abused, and dismissed by a system that blamed them for the problems they were trying to solve.

This important follow-up to *The Courage to Teach* includes a Foreword by Parker Palmer and is written by ordinary, brown-bag-toting teachers who have used his principles in their classrooms to overcome day-to-day obstacles and once again find joy in their work. Their warm, practical, funny, and moving true stories provide encouragement and hope to teachers everywhere in their battle to reclaim the courage to teach.

SAM M. INTRATOR (Northampton, MA), the son of two public school teachers, is assistant professor of education and child study at Smith College. For many years he was an inner city high school teacher.

[Price subject to change]